Report Writing Fundamentals for Police and Correctional Officers

Report Writing Fundamentals for Police and Correctional Officers

JAMES E. GUFFEY

Upper Saddle River, New Jersey 07458

Library of Congress Cataloging-in-Publication Data

Guffey, James E.
   Report writing fundamentals for police and correctional officers / James E. Guffey.
    p. cm.
   Includes index.
   ISBN 0-13-110272-9
   1. Police reports—Authorship. 2. Report writing. 1. Title.

HV7936.R53G84 2005
808'.066363—dc22

2003069040

Executive Editor: Frank Mortimer, Jr.
Assistant Editor: Korrine Dorsey
Marketing Manager: Tim Peyton
Editorial Assistant: Barbara Rosenberg
Managing Editor: Mary Carnis
Production Liaison: Brian Hyland
Production Editor: Janet Bolton
**Director of Manufacturing
  and Production:** Bruce Johnson
Manufacturing Manager: Ilene Sanford

Manufacturing Buyer: Cathleen Petersen
Design Director: Cheryl Asherman
Senior Design Coordinator: Miguel Ortiz
Cover Design: Carey Davies
Cover Art: Matthew Klein/CORBIS
Composition: Integra
Electronic Art Creation: Integra
Printing and Binding: Banta, Harrisonburg
Proofreader: Maine Proofreading Services
Copy Editor: Maine Proofreading Services

Pearson Prentice Hall™ is a trademark of Pearson Education, Inc.
Pearson® is a registered trademark of Pearson plc
Prentice Hall® is a registered trademark of Pearson Education, Inc.

Pearson Education LTD.
Pearson Education Australia PTY, Limited
Pearson Education Singapore, Pte. Ltd.
Pearson Education North Asia Ltd.
Pearson Education Canada, Ltd.
Pearson Educacion de Mexico, S.A. de C.V.
Pearson Education—Japan
Pearson Education Malaysia, Pte. Ltd.
Pearson Education, Upper Saddle River, New Jersey

10 9 8 7 6 5 4 3 2 1
ISBN 0-13-110272-9

To my wife, Natalya; my sons, Derek and Zachary;
and my daughter, Melissa

Contents

Preface

Report Writing Fundamentals for Police and Correctional Officers is designed to review the basics of English for the many students, police, and correctional officers who find that their skills in this area are in need of improvement. Even the best English writers will tell you that an occasional review is helpful. This text adds to the review several exercises to practice your newly acquired skills. Those finding this textbook useful would be:

- Basic police academies.
- Correctional academies.
- Police in-service report writing classes.
- Correctional in-service report writing classes.
- Colleges offering both a police and a correctional report writing class that wish to combine the two into one class.
- Colleges offering both a police and a correctional report writing class that wish to keep the classes separate yet find a common text for both classes.
- Police and correctional supervisory personnel who wish to have a reference when evaluating reports.
- Police or correctional officers who, for whatever reason, are unable to take a report writing class but who wish to improve their skills by self-study. The programmed text format of this textbook makes this possible.

ORGANIZATION OF THE BOOK

This book is divided into two sections. Section I is designed for those users who want to go directly into writing sample reports. Section II is designed for those users who want to combine a review of basic English grammar and construction with Section I.

Acknowledgments

Being my first published book, I would like to acknowledge the professional assistance of several people who made this dream of mine come true. First, I want to thank the staff at Prentice Hall who saw the need for my book and agreed to publish it. In particular I want to thank Frank Mortimer and his wife; Korrine Dorsey who kept me on Schedule; and the others "behind the scene" who contributed. I particularly want to thank Janet Bolton, my editor, who worked tirelessly to make sure all the "i's" were dotted and "t's" were crossed. I would like to acknowledge my friend and colleague, Dr. P.J. Ortmeier of Grossmont College, who assured me that my book would be an improvement over many currently used in community colleges. I would also like to thank the following for reviewing *Report Writing Fundamentals for Police and Correctional Officers*: Suzann W. Barr, University of Arkansas at Little Rock, Little Rock, AR; Alex del Carmen, University of Texas—Arlington, Arlington TX; Gary J. Margolis, University of Vermont Department of Police Services, Burlington, VT; Alan Marston, Southern Maine Community College, Portland, ME; Michael J. Palmiotto, Wichita State University, Wichita, KS; Emil A. Radosevich, Albuquerque Technical Vocational Institute, Albuquerque, NM; Jeffrey L. Schrink, Indiana State University, Terre Haute, IN. Finally, I would like to acknowledge Dr. George Payton, professor emeritus of Evergreen College, who allowed me to be a co-author with him and thus convinced me I could publish on my own.

Jim Guffey
National University
jguffey@nu.edu

About the Author

Dr. Jim Guffey began his career as a police officer for the city of Oakland, California, in 1973. After almost 13 years of police service and nearing the completion of a Ph.D. in Public Administration, he decided to return to active U.S. Army service as a Major and an Assistant Professor of Military Science at the University of California–Davis. At the completion of this 4-year tour, he taught for 5 years in the Administration of Justice Department at California State University–Hayward. From 1996 to 2000, he was the Director of the Public Safety Division at Porterville College in Porterville, California. Currently, he is an Associate Professor of Criminal Justice at National University in La Jolla, California. He is co-author with Emeritus Professor Dr. George Payton of two other textbooks: *Peace Officer's Guide to Criminal Law* and *Concepts of California Criminal Law*. Dr. Guffey can be contacted at (916) 855-4109 or jguffey@nu.edu.

Report Writing Fundamentals for Police and Correctional Officers

Report Writing Fundamentals and Sample Report Writing Exercises

This section is designed for those users who do not want to review the basics of English grammar, syntax, and construction. However, after completing the report writing sample exercises, you or your instructor or both may find the review of Section II to be helpful.

Introduction

1

The author decided to write this textbook for public safety report writers and students in order to fill a need for a combined public safety/report writing text. In the California community college system, those community colleges that offer a public safety curriculum generally have a law enforcement communications course and a correctional communications course. Some community colleges have combined the two into a public safety communications course. The author believes this textbook fills the need to have one textbook for each of these courses.

In addition, this textbook can serve as a supplement in basic police and correctional academies. It can also be used in any 24- to 40-hour in-service/professional classes that are mandated by state police and correctional officer standards and training commissions or by separate agencies. Finally, this textbook is written in a programmed text format so that individual police or correctional officers can purchase the textbook as a "carry-along" self-help textbook to assist with writing reports.

Criminal justice professionals cite report writing as the single most problematic area among police and correctional officers. This textbook can make every public safety report writer a much better report writer. It is flexible in that there is a comprehensive review of English grammar, construction, punctuation, and style, which can serve as a review or as a primary section of the textbook. Community college instructors may find that even though a basic English composition and grammar course is required of their administration of justice students, a review of this material is always a good practice. Personally, the author occasionally refers to "shelf texts" on English grammar and style to be reminded of good usage, and he is confident this occurs with most experienced writers.

GENDER REFERENCE

Throughout this textbook, the pronoun *he* is used rather than the clumsy *he/she* pronoun combination. He will *always* refer to both male and female, unless *she* is specifically used.

DEFINITION OF A REPORT

A report is the factual information of an event recorded on a form that provides the official record of an event for purposes of testimony, civil liability, retrieval, and posterity.

Types of Reports in Public Safety

Police and Security	*Corrections*	*Fire/Rescue*
Arrest	Arrest	Arson
Auto Theft	Crime	Incident
Clearance	Evidence	Log
Crime	Incident	Medical Emergency
Incident	Inmate Rules	Suspicious Fire
Infraction	Log	
Memorandums		
Missing Persons		
Fire		
Traffic Accident Statements		
Outside Agency Statements		

Administrative Reports

Both police and correctional agencies must prepare administrative reports. These can range from standard policy for agencies to reports for the next level in the administrative hierarchy. These reports often are summaries or findings of a critical incident. A few examples of critical incidents are (1) an officer-involved shooting, (2) a high-speed chase resulting in an injury or fatality, (3) a crowd-control situation wherein excessive force is alleged, (4) a hostage situation with most any resolution, (5) an inmate disturbance or lockdown, (6) the use of deadly force by correctional officers, and (7) a prison escape. This is by no means an exhaustive list, but these examples portray the types of administrative reports that result from a high-profile incident.

Administrative reports can be subpoenaed at subsequent hearings or trials, and they can result in costly litigation or can certainly shed a negative light on the agency, if they are not written well and do not capture all of the facts. Generally, police or correctional officers who begin their careers as good investigative report writers will naturally be good administrative report writers when they advance to the administrative ranks of their agencies. As a matter of fact, good investigative report writing is one of the skills focused on when agencies select police or correctional officers for promotion.

BASICS OF A GOOD REPORT

Quality Writing

Poor report writing skills reflect negatively in many ways. They are time-consuming to read and thus waste valuable law enforcement and correctional resources. It is embarrassing to the officers who are poor report writers. Poorly written reports are the single most frequent cause of criminal cases being lost because prosecutors will not charge. When prosecutors do charge poorly written cases, the cases are frequently lost to pretrial motions or at trial. Finally, poorly written reports may result in civil suits against the officer and his department. This book was designed to improve the quality of reports being written by all police and correctional officers and to prepare the pre-service administration of justice student to become an excellent report writer.

Public safety reports are unique, and they must conform to certain standards. There are six universally accepted writing qualities that these reports must have:

1. *Accurate.* It is very important that public safety reports are accurate. There are times when, if reporting citizens lie to the reporting officer, a report may be unintentionally inaccurate. This may be beyond the ability of the officer to control, without contradicting evidence. The key or operative term here is facts gleaned from skilled interviewing combined with corroborating evidence.

2. *Clear.* Have you ever heard of gobbledygook or terms popularized by politicians such as "misspoke," "untruth" or "half truth"? Politicians are masters at being unclear. But we do not hold politicians to the same accuracy as is expected from public safety officers. So public safety officers must use words that convey instant meaning to the reader. This also means that their grammar must be impeccable because misplaced modifiers, improperly used antecedents, etc., can cause confusion and make a report unclear.

3. *Complete.* If you have written a research paper, you may remember how hard it was to narrow a topic down to a workable title. You may, for example, want to write a report on the history of the FBI in 10 to 12 typed pages. You might be able to do this, but the report would certainly be incomplete. For a research paper, this may be acceptable. However, if you are a police officer writing a crime report about a burglary for which you have someone in custody, you cannot be incomplete. It would be the equivalent of an "F" paper if you so much as omitted one element of the *corpus delicti* or the probable cause for your arrest.

4. *Concise.* In the same scenario as above, you may use 3 of your 12 pages in discussing the life of J. Edgar Hoover, just to fill space. In the crime report, on the other hand, if you were to

write several pages discussing the suspect's criminal background, this would be superfluous and add nothing to the facts of the incident. You must be concise; tell the complete story in as few words as possible.

5. *Factual.* Using the research paper as an example again, you may also credit the FBI with the arrest and prosecution of gangster Al Capone. This would not be factual and could suggest that you did not conduct research for your paper. For example, in a hypothetical burglary, let us say you could not find a forced point of entry. You conclude that the owner must have left the door unlocked. Subsequently the owner testifies that he remembers locking his door. You can easily see how this factual testimony can give the defense attorney some tremendously impeaching cross-examination.

6. *Objective.* You may remember when your teachers told you a test would be 100 percent objective rather than subjective. You might have thought, "Oh no, now I can't overwhelm him with my creative writing." You had to know the right answer from among four or five choices. The police report is like an objective test: It must have all the right answers or be as close to perfectly correct as is humanly possible under the circumstances. For example, if you are taking a rape report from a woman you know to be a prostitute, you cannot discount her story before you begin a preliminary interview. If you do, your personal prejudice has now influenced the investigation and you are no longer being objective. By the same token, you cannot allow emotion or opinion to enter into your report.

Note Taking

Notes are the "grist" for your report. When a public safety officer responds to a call, he may not have his report forms handy, and he often does not want to have them with him. Public safety officers often face danger and must have both hands free for defense. Therefore, every public safety officer should carry a notebook that fits comfortably in the duty shirt pocket. This seems to be the best location to carry the notebook because it is easily accessible. The notebook itself can become the best evidence and hence be relied on quite heavily in court. Loose-leaf notes allow the officer to replace, remove, or easily alter notes, and this can create a negative impression when the officer is questioned by defense attorneys in open court. For this reason most prosecutors prefer either spiral or bound notebooks.

Notes are evidence and are subject to subpoena. For this reason, officers should not include matters of a personal nature. There should be some system of separating cases within the notebook. This can be done using a title page. An example is shown below:

Case: Robbery (211 P.C.)
Complainant: Jones

Report Number: 98-00000001
Date: 1/1/04
Pages in Notebook: 10–21

The title page would not have a number; every subsequent page would. By using a systematic record-keeping method in your notebooks, you gain credibility with both the prosecutor and the defense attorney.

You may also use the same notebook for other purposes. You may record information about suspicious automobiles or people on your beat or geographical area, and you may record information given out during roll call. In these cases, your title page could be:

Suspicious Vehicles
Date: 2/3/04
Pages: 22–23

Roll Call Information
Date: 2/3/04
Pages: 24–26

A variety of information can be included on the first page of the notes, and this is often dictated by agency policy. Examples of information on the first page are as follows: shift, area or beat, partner's name, weather conditions, and nature of this assignment (e.g., special assignment, stakeout, undercover).

How Are Notes Taken?

The best method to use is to take notes chronologically; using this system, you can more easily transfer data from your notes to the final report. Using this method, you might have the following:

2115: I spoke with complainant Jones. Statement was taken.
2150: I called for evidence technician.
2200: Evidence Technician Williams arrived.
2210: Technician Williams began to collect physical evidence.
2215: I prepared the robbery report
2255: I cleared the scene.

Listening. Listening is the key to taking complete and accurate notes. You want to get as many details in your notes as possible without actually writing a report. The purpose of notes is the same as that of an outline for a research paper. It becomes the "skeleton" from which you expand and include all of the details in the final report. Therefore, the more details you get into this skeleton, the more accurate your report will be.

For security officers, notes become even more important because a security officer may never have to write a formal report. As a security officer makes his tour or security check of the building or installation, he should use the same chronological note-taking procedure. An example is shown below:

2200: Logged on for duty
2210: Began security rounds
2215: Checked east end of warehouse—negative results
2230: Checked offices of president/vice president—secure
2245: Checked bathrooms—negative results
2315: Checked alarm system—set
0600: Off duty

In summary, note taking is the essence of good report writing. All officers should be doing it.

COMMON ABBREVIATIONS/ACRONYMS FOR NOTE TAKING

Abbreviations/acronyms should be used for purposes of note taking; however, most agency guidelines *do not* recommend using them for report narratives. This should be your practice.

ADW	Assault with a deadly weapon
AKA	Also known as
AMT	Amount
APPROX	Approximately
APT	Apartment
ARR	Arrest
ATT	Attempt or attached
ATTN	Attention
BKG	Booking
BLDG	Building
CAPT/CPT	Captain
CCW	Carrying concealed weapon
CMDR	Commander
COMP	Complainant
CPL	Corporal
DEF	Defendant
DEPT	Department
DMV	Department of Motor Vehicles
DOA	Dead on arrival
DOB	Date of birth
E/B	Eastbound
ETC	And so forth
FED	Federal
FI	Field interview
FTO	Field training officer
GOA	Gone on arrival
HBD	Has been drinking
HGT	Height
HQ	Headquarters
INV	Investigation

JUV	Juvenile
L/F	Left front
LIC	License
LKA	Last known address
L/R	Left rear
LT	Lieutenant
MAJ	Major
N/B	Northbound
NCIC	National Crime Information Center
NFD	No further description
NMI	No middle initial
OFC/OFF	Officer
PC	Penal code or probable cause
POE	Point of entry or point of exit
QTY	Quantity
R/F	Right front
R/O	Reporting officer
R/R	Right rear
RTE	Route
S/B	Southbound
SGT	Sergeant
SUBJ	Subject
SUSP	Suspect
U.S.	United States
VC	Vehicle code
VEH	Vehicle
VICT	Victim
VIN	Vehicle identification number
WAR	Warrant
W/B	Westbound
WIT	Witness

AUDIENCES FOR A REPORT

You should be aware that, in addition to those within your agency and other agencies, there will be many criminal justice professionals reading your reports. Every report begins with the writer. Next in the progression will be a supervisor who will read your report for errors of all types. If your report gets to an investigator, he will read it. Internally, these professionals will make written and mental comments about your writing. Poor report writing could be reflected in your evaluations and affect your career progression, as discussed earlier under Administrative Reports.

Outside Your Agency

Below are some outside people/agencies that may read your report and how they might evaluate it.

ATTORNEYS

Prosecutors are looking for probable cause, elements of the crime, evidence collected, and chargeability of the crime. They will not be understanding of your errors or sloppiness. Defense attorneys are looking for the same factors as the prosecutor, but they will be seeking any avenue to attack your report and thus your credibility. This can be something as simple as conflicting dates or times.

COURTS

Appellate courts are looking for evidence to reverse or sustain a case on appeal. If there is any doubt about your wording, they are most likely to find in favor of reversal. Remember: You will not be allowed to go before appeals courts to defend your report.

JURORS

Jurors are unpredictable, but they will understand and support officer testimony based on well-written reports. A defense attorney who cross-examines and points outs weaknesses in your report may sway the jurors to discredit most of your testimony.

MEDIA

It often seems as if the media are looking for any reason to make you and your agency look bad. Your report will be their basis.

QUIZ

1. The six basics of a good report are:

   _____

   _____

   _____

   _____

   _____

   _____

2. True   False   Field notes are not subject to subpoena.

3. True   False   It is best to separate notes with a title page.

4. The best note-taking method is to take your notes _____.

5. True   False   Note taking is less important for security officers.

2

Writing in the Active Voice

FRAME 1

This is an instructional package about writing in the active voice. Numbered frames present instructional material. At the conclusion of the instructional material, you will be asked to respond to questions or to do other activities that cause you to apply the information. Answers to the questions are found at the end of each chapter. Try to complete the frame questions without checking for the answers.

Note: If you are not familiar with the past participle verb form, you should take time to review Chapter 7 before starting this chapter.

FRAME 2

This programmed learning material will do these things: (1) teach you what the grammatical term *voice* means, (2) teach you how to identify active and passive voice, (3) teach you about the relationship of tense and voice, (4) point out the reasons for not using the passive voice, (5) point out the virtues of active voice, (6) teach permissible uses of passive voice, (7) teach you how to convert passive voice to active voice, and (8) provide general advice on the topic of voice.

FRAME 3

The word *voice* usually refers to a sound made by a speaker. In its grammatical sense, it refers to the way in which writers use verbs in sentences. When the subject of a sentence acts or performs, the verb is in the active voice. When the subject of the sentence receives action, the verb is in the passive voice. Note these examples:

Active voice: The cow ate the grass.
Passive voice: The grass was eaten by the cow.

Supply the correct word in the blanks for the next two items.

1. If the subject performs the action, the verb is in the _____ voice.

2. If the subject receives the action, the verb is in the _____ voice.

FRAME 4

Classify the following sentences as to whether the subject performs or receives action.

1. Henry was called Harold by his mother. _____

2. The veterinarian vaccinated the cat. _____

3. The cat was vaccinated by the veterinarian _____

4. Mabel placed a wreath at the monument. _____

5. In the evening we met for social hour. _____

6. Sheila classifies the responses. _____

FRAME 5

Let's apply what you have learned. Identify the following sentences as active or passive. Use the rule about the subject performing or receiving action.

1. The janitor lives in Greenville. _____

2. He ate the whole pie. _____

3. The mouse was eaten by the cat. _____

4. She rolled the ball down the alley. _____

FRAME 6

There are two ways to identify passive voice; one is by the rule just discussed. Also, you can identify passive voice by the combination of a two-part verb where one part of the verb is a form of the verb *to be* and the other part of the two-part verb is a past participle form of another verb. (More on this later.)

Which of the following are valid rules for identifying passive voice? (Respond valid or not valid in the blanks.)

1. If the subject of a sentence receives the action, the sentence is in the passive voice. _____

2. If there is no action verb in the sentence, it is in the passive voice. _____

3. If the sentence has a form of the verb *to be* and a past participle form of a verb, the sentence is in the passive voice. _____

FRAME 7

We said that you can identify passive voice by the presence of a form of a *to be* verb combined with the past participle form of another verb. This may require more explanation. The verb *be* or *to be* is perhaps the most common verb in the English language. Here are the different forms of that verb: am, are, is, was, were, be, being, and been.

Which of the following are *not* forms of the verb *to be*? (Circle those verbs that are not forms of the verb *to be*.)

being   are   was   has   is   be

am   had   have   be   were   been

FRAME 8

Sentences in passive voice combine a form of the verb *to be* with a past participle form of another verb. The table below shows the different forms that some verbs can take. Study the table; note that the first three verbs change in the same, or regular, way; these verbs are regular verbs. Note that the last three change in different, or irregular, ways; such verbs are irregular verbs.

Present Form	*Past Form*	*Past Participle Form*
discover	discovered	discovered
work	worked	worked
believe	believed	believed
know	knew	known
give	gave	given
begin	began	begun

FRAME 9

To understand passive voice construction, you need to know about past participle forms of verbs. Here is a system for identifying present, past, and past participle forms of any verb: (1) "Today I *go*." (2) "Yesterday I *went*." (3) "I have *gone*."

By determining the form of the verb that goes into the construction "Today I _____," you can find the present form of the verb; by finding the form of the verb that fits into the construction "Yesterday I _____," you can find the past form of the verb; and by finding the form of the verb that fits into the construction "I have _____," you can find the past participle form of the verb.

Use this system to fill in the blanks below.

Present Form	Past Form	Past Participle Form
1. Today I _____.	Yesterday I _____.	I have <u>thought</u>.
2. Today I _____.	Yesterday I <u>carried</u>.	I have _____.
3. Today I _____.	Yesterday I <u>hid</u>.	I have _____.

FRAME 10

Let us review. We said that a second method of identifying passive voice was the combination of a form of the verb *to be* along with a past participle form of another verb. Identify the combinations below that indicate passive voice.

1. has made _____

2. was seen _____

3. are frozen _____

4. will do _____

5. is lost _____

6. was eaten _____

7. been lost _____

FRAME 11

We will give some additional instruction on this topic. Sometimes one or more words will intervene between a form of the verb *to be* and the past participle form of the other verb. For example:

The fence was seriously damaged.

Note that the word "seriously" intervenes between the *to be* verb and the past participle form of the verb, "damaged." Pay attention to this possibility, and select the constructions that indicate passive voice.

1. The samples were carefully packaged. _____

2. Janet had always preferred rice over potatoes. _____

3. The dog is seriously injured. _____

4. Ken had carefully distinguished between red and scarlet. _____

FRAME 12

We have taught you two rules. The first rule said to decide whether the subject of the sentence acted or received the action. If the subject acted, then the sentence was in active voice. If the subject received the action, the sentence was in passive voice. The second rule asks you to identify the presence of a *to be* verb combined with the past participle form of another verb. Use either or both rules to identify the following sentences as active or passive.

1. The player was defeated by a small margin. _____

2. Margaret can manage the problem. _____

3. The winner was ridden by Pat Casey. _____

4. Tiger was consumed by jealousy when the new cat arrived. _____

5. Harold has carefully completed the lesson. _____

FRAME 13

If you did not get all five items correct, go back and review frames 1 through 10.

Tense has some relation to the problems of passive voice (but not much). Tense is a grammatical term relating to time and completion of action. Passive voice occurs frequently in the past tense but can occur in other tenses. Note these examples:

Past tense—The bridge was finished on time.

Present tense—The bridge is now finished.

Future tense—The bridge will be finished.

Past perfect tense—The bridge had been finished.

Present perfect tense—The bridge has been finished.

Future perfect tense—The bridge will have been finished.

Answer the following questions with *true* or *false*.

1. All six examples above are in passive voice. _____

2. Passive voice occurs only in the past tense. _____

3. Passive voice occurs most frequently in the past tense. _____

FRAME 14

Here is a quick quiz on material covered so far.

1. The grammatical term _____ deals with whether the subject of a sentence acts or receives action.

2. The words *am, are, was,* and *is* are all different forms of the verb _____.

3. Which of the following verbs is in the past participle form? ring, rang, rung _____.

4. Which of the following verbs is the past participle form of the verb? blown, blow, blew _____.

FRAME 15

If you missed questions 3 and 4, go back and review frames 6, 7, and 8.

If you have completed all of the frames to this point, you should be able to identify passive voice constructions. Let's consider reasons why you should write in the active voice. The active voice tells the reader who is talking; it tells the reader who is giving instructions or who is acting. Consider some of the problems in this sentence written in the passive voice: "Space will be allocated on an available basis." The problem with the foregoing example sentence is that it hides the actor. We (the readers) want to know who will allocate space. We want to know whom to talk to if we want space.

What information is absent in this sentence written in the passive voice?

1. The process for vulcanizing rubber was invented in 1839. _____

FRAME 16

A second reason for using the active voice is efficiency. Note the difference in the two sentences that follow:

Passive voice: The total should be divided by the number of cases.

Active voice: Divide the total by the number of cases.

1. How many words are in the passive voice sentence?
   _____

2. How many words are in the active voice sentence?
   _____

FRAME 17

The third reason for using the active voice is that it is direct, natural, forceful, and easy to understand.

Passive: The index should be consulted before it is decided if a word should be included.

Active: Before you decide to include a word, consult the index.

1. Which of the above sentences is direct and easy to understand? _____

FRAME 18

A fourth reason for using active voice is that all police departments and correctional agencies require that reports be written in the active voice. Because police and correctional writing must be concise, it is even more important to write in the active voice.

In the spaces below, list the four reasons for writing in the active voice.

1. _____
2. _____
3. _____
4. _____

FRAME 19

Which of the four reasons (from among the four shown above) is most applicable for changing the following sentence to active voice?

1. The new equipment has been received and will be issued to all public safety personnel.

_____

FRAME 20

So far you have learned to identify active and passive voice constructions; also, you should know why active voice is preferable. Now we will explain how to change passive constructions to active. Consider this: "The old building was condemned by the city in 1978." A simple way to change this passive construction is to make city the subject of the sentence; you can do this by changing the word order. By changing the word order, you put the actor in the first part of the sentence, which is usually the best place for it: "The city condemned the old building in 1978."

Use this technique to transform the following sentence to active voice.

1. The old boss was remembered by most of the employees.

_____

FRAME 21

Here is another technique for converting passive voice to active voice. This technique is applicable when giving instructions or orders. Consider this example in the passive voice: "The colon should be placed at the beginning of a list." Convert such a sentence to active voice by using the understood *you* as the subject of the sentence. (You) "Place a colon at the beginning of a list." The understood, but not written, subject of the sentence is *you*.

Use this technique to convert the following sentence to active voice.

1. All of the new employees will be oriented prior to assignment.

_____

FRAME 22

Here is still another technique for converting passive voice to active voice. Sometimes you can convert a sentence to active voice by supplying a subject when the actor is hidden. Consider this example written in the passive voice: "After you have been enrolled in the course, you will be assigned to a classroom." The example sentence contains two uses of the passive voice—one in the introductory clause and one in the main clause. We will convert the construction to active voice by supplying subjects that identify the actor (we have italicized the supplied subjects): "After *we* enroll you in the course, *we* will assign you to a classroom."

Use this technique to transform the following sentence to active voice.

1. After the harvest is gathered, workers will be paid according to weight of produce gathered.

_____

FRAME 23

Another technique for changing passive voice to active voice is the frequent use of I, we, names of persons, or specific objects as the subjects of sentences. Instead of saying "It is requested," you can say, "Officer Jones wants you to . . . ," or you can say, "I want you to do it this way."

Use this technique to transform the following passive voice sentence to active voice.

1. On the request of the patrol captain, you are ordered to report to his office for a special assignment.

_____

FRAME 24

Rewrite the following sentences in the active voice.

1. Meetings were held by the mayor so that questions could be answered.

_____

_____

2. All of the pay cards should be collected and delivered to the city's Finance Office.

_____

_____

FRAME 25

Rewrite the following sentences in the active voice.

1. The material can be ordered through the catalog department.

_____

_____

2. This office has been tasked by the director to inventory all of the orders that have been filed since the department was established.

_____

_____

FRAME 26

Now we will consider some permissible uses of the passive voice. We said earlier that the passive voice hides the actor. Sometimes the actor is unknown so we use the passive voice. Here is an example: "The Maple Street branch of the First National Bank was robbed this afternoon." In the example sentence, we do not know who the robbers were so the use of passive voice is permissible. However, it is possible to change the sentence to active voice: "A person or persons unknown robbed the Maple Street branch of the First National Bank this afternoon."

Are the following sentences appropriate for the passive voice?

1. The evidence was turned in to Property by Officer Williams.
   _____

2. The doors were removed from the cell. _____

FRAME 27

In some instances, we use the passive voice because we want to de-emphasize the subject or actor. See this example: "The new building was named after President Nixon." In the example sentence, we do not much care what committee decided on the name. Instead, we want to emphasize the name of the building, not the naming agency.

Is the following sentence more appropriate for active or passive voice?

1. The new wing of the capitol building in Sacramento was named in honor of Cesar Chavez. _____

FRAME 28

Now we will begin a series of reviews. We began by saying that a sentence is in active voice if the subject performs the action; it is in passive voice if the subject receives the action.

Classify the following sentences as active or passive.

1. Peter has worked there for three months. _____

2. The disk was copied from the master copy. _____

3. The kidney was removed by the surgeon. _____

4. This general order was written by the chief of police. _____

FRAME 29

There are two ways to identify passive voice. One is by deciding whether the subject performs the action or receives the action. The other method is by identifying the presence of a form of the verb _____, combined with the _____ form of another verb.

FRAME 30

Let us review the information about past participle forms of verbs. We used a system or procedure to determine the present, past, and past participle forms of verbs: "Today I _____." "Yesterday I _____." "I have _____."

Use this system to complete the table below:

Present Form	Past Form	Past Participle Form
_____	went	_____
_____	_____	done
know	_____	_____
_____	cleaned	_____

FRAME 31

We said that sometimes other words intervene between a form of the verb *to be* and the past participle form of another verb. The intervening words do not change the classification rules.

Classify the following sentences as active or passive voice.

1. Fred was often selected for leadership positions. _____

2. The suspect was carefully questioned. _____

    3. We have always wished for good fortune. _____

    4. The break can be repaired. _____

FRAME 32

We said that passive voice is common in the past tense but possible in other tenses. There are at least four reasons for using active voice:

1. Active voice tells the reader who is communicating, acting, or doing.
2. Active voice is more efficient.
3. Active voice is direct, forceful, natural, and easy to understand
4. Police and corrections reports must be in the active voice, except for the exceptions noted above.

FRAME 33

You can reconstruct passive voice sentences by use of these techniques:

1. Reverse the sentence order and put the actor at the beginning of the sentence.
2. If giving directions, write instructions using the understood subject *you.*
3. Provide a subject when the subject is vague or unstated.
4. Use specific pronouns such as *I* or *we* as subjects of sentences; use names or specific objects as the subjects of sentences.

FRAME 34

In general, it is good advice to avoid the passive voice. However, there are some situations where passive voice is permissible. Passive voice is permissible if the actor is unknown or if the actor is not important.

    Frame 35 is a test of some of the things you have learned.

FRAME 35

Classify sentences 1–3 as active or passive.

1. John has always tried harder than Kelly. _____

2. The project was completed before the deadline. _____

3. She reminded me of my sister Helen. _____

Rewrite sentences 4–6 in active voice.

4. The comma should be placed before the word.

   _____

   _____

5. The old dog was abandoned by the owner.

   _____

   _____

6. This office has been tasked to prepare a training report.

   _____

   _____

Classify sentences 7–9 as appropriate or not appropriate for passive voice.

7. A speech was delivered by Senator Green. _____

8. The Olympic Games were first held in 1896. _____

9. One of the guns was taken from the gun rack. _____

QUIZ

1. When the subject of the sentence acts or performs, the verb is in the _____ _____ .

2. When the subject of the sentence receives action, the verb is in the _____.

Classify the following sentences as to whether the subject performs or receives the action.

3. Officer Jones was called to the scene by his sergeant.

   _____

4. Officer Williams chased the suspect. _____

5. The fleeing suspect was pursued by Officer O'Reilly, who drove dangerously fast. _____

6. The poorly written report was returned to Officer Holden by his sergeant, Joe Friday. _____

Fill in the blanks of the following questions.

7. There are two ways to identify passive voice. The first way is to ask yourself, "Is the subject of the sentence _____ or _____ the action of the verb?"

8. The second way to identify passive voice is to determine if the verb is in two parts: One part is a form of the verb _____, and the other part is a _____ form of another verb.

9. The different forms of the verb *to be* are _____, _____, _____, _____, _____, _____, and _____.

Answer the following multiple-choice questions.

10. Which of the following is in the past participle form?
    a. believe
    b. know
    c. work
    d. discovered

11. Which of the following is in the past participle form?
    a. pursue
    b. arrest
    c. begun
    d. interrogate

12. Which of the following is a combination of a *to be* verb plus a part participle form of another verb?
    a. was seen
    b. will do
    c. has made
    d. none of the above

Using the rules you have been taught, classify the following sentences as active or passive.

13. The trace evidence was carefully packaged by the evidence technician. _____

14. The pit bull was seriously injured by a round from Officer Zimmerman's handgun. _____

15. Officer Wong has always preferred patrol over investigation._____

16. Sergeant Good is being divorced by his wife of ten years. _____

Complete or answer the following questions.

17. The grammatical term _____ deals with whether the subject of a sentence acts or receives action.

18. The words *am, are, was,* and *is* are all different forms of the verb _____.

19. Which of the following verbs is in the past participle form? ring, rang, rung

20. Which of the following verbs is in the past participle form of the verb? blown, blow, blew

21. There are three reasons why we must use the *active voice* in writing reports. Which of the following is *not* a reason?
    a. The active voice tells the reader who is doing the action.
    b. The active voice is efficient.
    c. The active voice is direct, natural, forceful, and easy to understand.
    d. The active voice allows the subject to receive the action rather than perform it.

22. "The handgun was found in the bushes." This is a passive voice sentence that defies which rule(s) above in question 21? (Answer with the multiple-choice letter.)

23. "The suspect was pursued by the police dog for ten blocks." This is a passive voice sentence that defies which rule(s) above? (Answer with the multiple-choice letter.)

24. "The penal code should be consulted before it is decided which section to use in your report." This is a passive voice sentence that defies which rule(s) above? (Answer with the multiple-choice letter.)

ANSWERS TO FRAMES

Frame 3
1. active
2. passive

Frame 4
1. receives
2. performs
3. receives
4. performs
5. performs
6. performs

Frame 5
1. active
2. active
3. passive
4. active

Frame 6
1. valid rule
2. not valid
3. valid rule

Frame 7

Not forms of the verb *to be:*
  4. has
  8. had
  9. have

Frame 9

Present	*Past*	*Past Participle*
think	thought	thought
carry	carried	carried
hide	hid	hidden

Frame 10

  2. was seen
  3. are frozen
  5. is lost
  6. was eaten
  7. been lost

Frame 11

  1. Sentences 1 and 3 are in the passive voice.

Frame 12

  1. passive
  2. active
  3. passive
  4. passive
  5. active

Frame 13

  1. true
  2. false
  3. true

Frame 14

  1. voice
  2. to be
  3. rung
  4. blown

Frame 15

  1. The sentence does not tell us who invented the vulcanizing process.

Frame 16

  1. Passive voice sentence—10 words
     Active voice sentence—8 words

Frame 17

  1. Sentence two is easier to understand.

Frame 18

  1. The active voice tells the reader who is acting, writing, doing, ordering, or wanting.
  2. The active voice is more efficient.
  3. The active voice is direct, natural, forceful, and easy to understand.
  4. All public safety agencies require that reports be written in the active voice.

Frame 19

  1. Reason 1 is the best answer, but reasons 2, 3, and 4 also apply.

Frame 20

  1. Most of the employees remembered their old boss.

Frame 21

  1. Orient all new employees prior to assignment.

Frame 22

  1. After you have gathered the harvest, we will pay you according to weight of produce.

Frame 23

  1. The patrol captain orders you to report to his office for a special assignment.

Frame 24

  1. The mayor held meetings to answer questions.
  2. Collect the pay cards and deliver them to the city's Finance Office.

Frame 25

  1. Order the material through the catalog department.

2. The director ordered us to inventory all orders on file since the establishment of the department.

Frame 26

1. not appropriate
2. appropriate

Frame 27

1. appropriate for passive voice

Frame 28

1. active
2. passive
3. passive
4. passive

Frame 29

1. to be   past participle

Frame 30

Present Form	Past Form	Past Participle Form
go	went	gone
do	did	done
know	knew	known
clean	cleaned	cleaned

Frame 31

1. passive
2. passive
3. active
4. passive

Frame 35

1. active
2. passive
3. active
4. Place the comma before the word.
5. The owner abandoned the old dog.
6. The chief of police (training unit) tasked us to prepare a training report.
7. not appropriate
8. appropriate
9. appropriate

Report Writing Mechanics, Style, and Editing

Now we are going to discuss the "how" of writing a good police report.

PROBABLE CAUSE TO STOP, DETAIN, ARREST, AND SEARCH IN YOUR REPORT

There is nothing more crucial to a police or corrections report than justifying a stop, detention, arrest, or search. In fact you may have all the probable cause or reasonable suspicion you need to actually justify your action, but if you do not articulate it properly in your report, you will probably not have your case charged. The purpose of this section is to discuss reasonable suspicion and probable cause and to explain how you develop these in your report.

Stop, Detention, Frisks, and Reasonable Suspicion

The standard for detention is frequently called reasonable suspicion. Reasonable suspicion requires that a "reasonable officer," based on experiences patrolling the area, would believe that some criminal activity is occurring. The landmark case in this area was *Terry v. Ohio* (392 U.S. 1). The Court authorized temporary detention for questioning if there are specific, articulable facts that lead a reasonable police officer to believe that criminal activity is occurring. The officer may consider information from victims, witnesses, and informants. Mere hunches are not enough. The officer may not stop a person based solely on the fact that the person is associating with known criminals or is at a location where criminal activity, such as drug sales, frequently occurs.

The Supreme Court, recognizing that it is frequently necessary to search a suspect for the safety of the officer, authorized protective searches during a temporary detention if the officer has a reasonable suspicion that the suspect is armed or dangerous. The limited search permitted in *Terry* is designed solely for the protection of the officer. There is no automatic right to search every person stopped. When authorized to conduct a limited search, the officer may pat down or frisk the suspect's outer clothing for weapons. This logically includes checking purses, backpacks, or items that the person is carrying. If the officer feels an object that he could reasonably surmise is a weapon, he may retrieve the suspicious object. If, in fact, the object seized is not a weapon, whatever was seized will still be admissible. On the other hand, if the officer feels something in the suspect's pocket that does not resemble a weapon, there is no right to retrieve it. The key here is that the officer must be able to write clearly in his report that the feel of the object was consistent with the shape and firmness of, for example, a handgun, a knife, brass knuckles, a sap, a wallet gun, or the many other types of weapons that could logically fit in a pocket, a crotch, a waistband, the small of the back, the lining of a coat, the armpit, or any other part of any outer clothing.

To further illustrate reasonable suspicion as well as stop and detain, I shall use the following example. You are an officer responding to a convenience store on a call of a disturbance. As you arrive, you see what appears to be the store owner chasing a man out of the store. The store owner stops and points to the man, who is still fleeing, and says, "Officer, he just robbed me." You realize that you must pursue the man or lose him, but you wish you had more information to go on. As you are running, you tell yourself that all you need is probable cause to believe a felony has been committed. You capture the man and place him under arrest for robbery at this point because you have the probable cause to believe that a robbery has been committed. You now return to the store where you talk with the store owner to establish the elements of robbery. Perhaps you learn that there was no fear on the store owner's part and no force used by the suspect. You now decide that this is only a theft (shoplifting). In your report you must establish your probable cause for the arrest. You determine that the elements of robbery did not exist; you did determine, however, that the elements of theft existed, giving you your probable cause for the citizen's arrest for shoplifting.

What if you decide that no crime has been committed? In this case you would release the suspect, and the arrest becomes only detention. Nevertheless, this must be thoroughly documented in your report because you want to have justification in case you are faced with a lawsuit and to show that this was only a detention for record-keeping purposes.

Below is a sample narrative of the example above:

> Store owner Jones observed a white juvenile male enter his store and go to the cigarette display. He was suspicious of the youth because the youth kept looking up from the cigarette display at him. He observed the youth grab several packs of cigarettes from the display and walk toward the exit. The store owner related that he yelled at the youth, "Don't take those cigarettes without paying for them." The store owner then came from behind the counter to apprehend the youth. According to the store owner, the youth began to run out of the store, and that is when the store owner encountered me. I observed the youth running, and I heard the store owner say, "Officer,

he just robbed me." I gave chase, captured the youth, and returned him to the store. The owner positively identified the youth as the one in the store who took the cigarettes without paying for them and fled. I had the store owner make a citizen's arrest for theft, and I took the youth into custody.

In this sample, the officer has established the probable cause to arrest, the elements of the crime of theft, and the justification for the arrest—citizen's arrest. All of these must be included in the report.

USE OF FIRST PERSON AND PERSONAL PRONOUNS AND NOUNS IN YOUR REPORT

When the author first became a police officer in the city of Oakland, California, in 1973, it was acceptable to write police reports in a nebulous third-person style. The author was always the "R/O." "R/O responded to 1138 E. 14th Street." "R/O observed the suspect running E/B in 4100 block of Foothill." "Witness #1 observed suspect #1 running W/B on Cypress Street in 2900 block." The author often wondered if the readers of these reports got whiplash from jerking their heads from these sentences back to the "witness" and "suspect" boxes on the face sheet. The other time-consuming choice was to spend several minutes on the face sheet memorizing who witness #1 and suspect #1 were.

After a couple of years of this, someone decided it was probably much better to use "I" instead of "R/O" and "witness Jones" for "witness #1" and "suspect Williams" for "suspect #1." This is what the author means by using personal nouns and pronouns. For example, you write, "Witness Jones observed suspect Williams running E/B in 4100 block of Foothill." In the next sentence, you can use personal pronouns because it is clear to whom the personal pronouns refer. The next sentence could be written, "*He* followed *him* for two blocks but lost *him* in the 2100 block of High Street."

Since this sentence follows the previous one, we know that *he* refers to witness Jones and *him* refers to suspect Williams. When using personal pronouns, however, always ask yourself, "Is it absolutely clear to whom these personal pronouns refer?"

AVOIDANCE OF JARGON, REPETITIOUS WORDS, AND STILTED WORDS IN YOUR REPORT

Having used the word "observed," the author would like to now introduce the new topic of areas of avoidance: jargon, repetitious words, and stilted words. Jargon is language that is specific to certain occupations that others may not recognize. In police work these would be penal and other code sections, radio codes, and police-specific abbreviations. For example, if you wrote in the introductory sentence to a report, "I was dispatched to take a 211 report at 9100 Olive Street," this would be police jargon. "I was dispatched to take a robbery report" is much clearer. Another example is, "When I arrived at the scene of the crime, the suspect was GOA." "When I arrived, the suspect was gone" is clearer.

Referring to "observed" again, the author wants to emphasize that you must use words that are simpler and more "visual." "I *saw* the suspect toss the bag." You can exit a vehicle, but it is more visual to say "I *stepped* out," or "I *bolted* out of the car in pursuit." *Webster's* defines bolt as "to move or spring suddenly." Doesn't this paint a more visual picture than exit? The key here is to constantly improve your vocabulary so that you can find more precise words to use in your sentences.

Give a simpler, more visual word for the commonly overused police words below.

1. advise   _____

2. approximately   _____

3. ascertain   _____

4. commenced   _____

5. detected   _____

6. indicated   _____

7. initiated   _____

8. informed   _____

9. inquired   _____

10. negative   _____

11. notified   _____

12. proceeded   _____

13. pursued   _____

14. related   _____

15. rendered   _____

16. stated   _____

17. transported   _____

18. utilized   _____

Stilted words are stiff or formal words. They are very similar to the repetitious words given in the previous exercise. The fine line of difference is that stilted words are usually spoken (particularly in court testimony). If we write stilted words in our reports, we are likely to use them in testimony. For example, the prosecutor asks, "What did you do next, Officer?" You respond, "I *apprehended* the suspect *pursuant* to penal code section 211 PC and placed him in the rear of my patrol vehicle." The italicized words are stilted. You may have actually written your report using these words and are testifying verbatim from your report. Let's see how we can simplify both the report and the testimony. Prosecutor: "What did you do next, Officer?" Officer: "I arrested the suspect for robbery." The jury can understand arrest, but apprehend may cloud their understanding of your intentions. Moreover, we have shortened the sentence from 21 words to 6. Why say something in 22 words that can be said in 6 and that is clearer to the reader/listener? Always look for ways to eliminate excessive, extraneous words and phrases. Another example of stilted words in a police report is, "The kidnapper failed to *ascertain* the facts necessary to *effectuate* the crime." Why not say, "The kidnapper did not plan the crime well." The sentence goes from 12 to 8 words, and we have eliminated the stilted words.

MECHANICS OF YOUR REPORT

If you remember from Chapter 1, we discussed note taking. You may want to go back to Chapter 1 for just a moment and look at this section again.

Once you have gathered your notes, you now want to write your report. Actually writing a report is very easy, if you use the fundamentals you have been taught. Here are the mechanics:

1. *Write in paragraphs.* You learned how to develop topic sentences. Introduce each paragraph with a topic sentence. This should be a transition idea.
2. *Be consistent in how you introduce your report.* "At about 2310, I was dispatched to investigate a burglary at 9230 D Street." This sentence tells the reader many of the necessary facts by which to understand the rest of your report.
3. *Write in chronological order.* Move from arriving at the crime scene to the next event and so on.
4. *Make sure you get all of the elements of all the charged crimes in your narrative.* Otherwise, the district attorney cannot charge them.
5. *Describe losses and recovered evidence in detail.*
6. *Make certain other participating officers are mentioned in your report, and prepare supplemental reports.* Tell briefly in your report what the other officers did.
7. *Always write your reports in the past tense.* You are always responding to something that has already happened.
8. *Never state your opinion in your report.*
9. *Indicate in your report what you were unable to accomplish and to which investigative unit you submitted the report.*

Your investigation will always involve a chain of events. You will respond to the scene and receive information from a victim.

This information will cause you to search for physical evidence or locate other witnesses and possibly the suspect. You follow each lead as far as you possibly can within the constraints of time and distance. This is the information you want to make sure you record chronologically in your report.

EDITING OF YOUR REPORT

There is one last step before you actually submit your report. You should edit your report for *all* of the things we have learned in this textbook. This is why it is important that you keep this textbook with you even when you are on duty. The more you read it and refer to it, the more you will be able to remember. Soon you may not need to refer to this book nearly as often.

The following figure shows some standard editing symbols with which you should become familiar. Do not be too lazy to edit your reports; then go back and rewrite them. The best report writers of the twenty-first century will have laptop computers and be experts in the use of word processing software. This will make rewrites much easier.

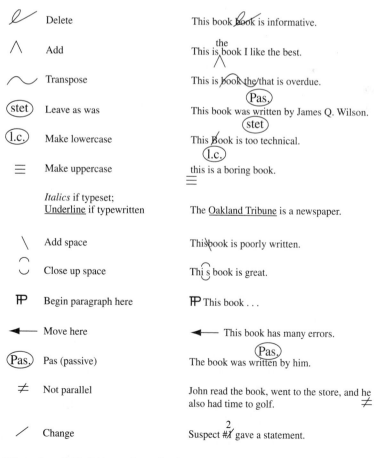

Standard Editing Symbols

If you do not feel comfortable using these editing symbols, you can use any method you like to indicate that you must make changes. The key is to always edit your report because you can be certain that it will read much better the second time.

The following are excerpts from reports that you are to edit. Using a red pen, edit each exercise and rewrite the excerpt.

EXERCISES

Exercise 1

While on patrol, southbound in the 1200 block of Broadway, I observed the defendant's vehicle travelling at a high rate of speed. The vehicle also periodically crossed over the centerline. I initiated a traffic stop and contacted Suspect Jones who after an initial identification procedure, it was determined that S-Jones had been drinking and was possibly drunk driving. S-Jones was ordered from the vehicle and was given a series of FSTs, which he failed. A check of warrants revealed the S-Jones was also wanted for investigation of burglary. S-Jones was booked on a deuce charge.

Rewrite Exercise 1 below:

_____

_____

_____

_____

_____

_____

_____

_____

_____

Exercise 2

I responded to 35th Ave and Foothill Blvd. reference minors drinking. Upon arrival, I observed a group of young males standing around a vehicle. The majority of the individuals were in possession of open containers of alcohol. Contact was made with S-Fernandes and it was subsequentally determined that he was under the age of 21. He was instructed to pour out the remaining beverage but became belligerant and uncooperative. At this time, it was decided to arrest S-Fernandes for violation of 25662 B & P.

Rewrite Exercise 2 below:

_____

_____

_____

_____

_____

_____

_____

_____

_____

Exercise 3

This officer and partner activated the overhead red and blue lights on our marked patrol vehicle and effected a vehicle stop on a late model two-door passenger car in the vicinity of Sobrante Park. Contact was made with the driver who identified himself as Roger Dale Clinton. Because this officer and partner feared the occupants of the vehicle might be armed, they were directed to exit the vehicle and take a position on the adjacent sidewalk. This officer then informed S-1 that he had reason to believe he might be in possession of an offensive weapon and that for this reason, this officer would would be conducting a pat-down search for any offensive weapons. A search of Clinton met with negative results. A passenger in the vehicle, however, made a furtive movement upon hearing of the impending search. He was immediately searched and a loaded .25-caliber pistol semi-auto was found in his pocket. This individual, identified as Lamont Smith, was read his rights which he agreed to waive and give a statement. S-1 then explained that the gun was handed to him by a third passenger Michael Gaylord in the car at the time of the traffic enforcement stop. It should be noted that S-1's explanation could not be true and that he was obviously lying. S-3 denied handing the gun to S-1, but implicated S-2 as the owner of the gun. A search was conducted of the vehicle at which time a ski mask was located, along with another gun, a .45-caliber Smith and Wesson. Was not loaded. All subjects were booked for outstanding warrants.

Rewrite Exercise 3 below:

_____

_____

_____

_____

_____

_____

_____

_____

_____

SAMPLE ANSWERS TO REPORT WRITING EXERCISES 1–3

Exercise 1

While on patrol, southbound in the 1200 block of Broadway, I saw . . . [Line 2 OK.] I stopped the vehicle for speeding and illegally crossing the centerline. I contacted the driver, Mr. Jones, who emitted a strong odor of alcohol. I asked Jones to come out of the vehicle, and I proceeded to give him a series of standard field sobriety tests. Jones failed all the tests, and I arrested him for driving under the influence of alcohol. A warrant check revealed he was also wanted for an outstanding burglary warrant.

Exercise 2

I responded to the intersection of 35th Ave. and Foothill Blvd. regarding minors drinking alcoholic beverages. [Line 2 is OK. Line 3 is OK.] I contacted suspect John Fernandes, and I determined from identification that he was under the age of 21. I instructed him to pour out the remaining beverage, but he became belligerent and uncooperative. I immediately decided to arrest suspect Fernandes for violation of Business and Professions Code Section 25662.

Exercise 3

My partner, Officer Thompson, and I stopped a late-model, two-door passenger car generally matching the description of a robbery vehicle broadcast earlier in the vicinity of Sobrante Park. Because we had reasonable cause to believe the occupants might be armed, we directed them to get out of the vehicle and take positions on the adjacent sidewalk. I contacted the driver, who identified himself as Roger Dale Clinton. I informed suspect Clinton that I had reason to believe he might be in possession of an offensive weapon, and I conducted a pat-down search of Clinton. I found no weapons.

Officer Thompson and I noticed that a passenger in the vehicle made a furtive movement upon hearing of the search of suspect Clinton. Officer Thompson immediately searched this suspect and found a loaded .25-caliber pistol in his right-front coat pocket. This suspect was identified as Lamont Smith. Officer Thompson read suspect Smith his rights, and Smith agreed to give a statement. Smith gave a written statement indicating that the third suspect, Michael Gaylord, handed him the gun at the time of the traffic stop. Suspect Gaylord denied handing the gun to suspect Smith and claimed Clinton was the owner of the gun. Officer Thompson and I handcuffed all three suspects and placed them in our patrol vehicle. We conducted a search of the suspect vehicle and found a ski mask and another handgun, a Smith and Wesson .45-caliber pistol. The gun was not loaded. We arrested all three suspects for possession of concealed weapons and outstanding warrants.

4

Writing Sample Police Reports

The following exercises begin with a simple police report and progress to a much more complicated multiple-offense report. There are five exercises. The first is a very uncomplicated burglary report. The second exercise progresses to a more complicated crime against a person. The third report is a complicated multiple-offense report, occurring over an entire evening and next morning. The fourth report is a missing person report, and the fifth report is a routine incident report.

You are to use the police report forms, which are included in this textbook as Appendix B. The author has prepared the first report based on the information given below (Report 1). This completed report will provide you with a model from which to prepare Reports 2 through 5. Your instructor will go over the report with you and explain the boxes. If time permits, your instructor can develop additional exercises and have you write additional reports. This is encouraged because the more you write, the better you will become. *Finally, the sample information for the four reports you will complete contains built-in errors that you must identify and correct in your reports.* Some hints: Remember that your report is being written in the past tense, watch for passive voice, and check for misspelled and unhyphenated words.

REPORT 1—BURGLARY

On April 14, 20XX, Mr. Pete Wilson arived at his residence at 4675 Ascot Drive, Anywhere, California 95555. The time was 9:35 P.M. Mr. Wilson found the front door of his home wide open. He could see that someone had hit the door with something very heavy as the door jamb was split and the deadbolt lock was lying on the floor. Mr. Wilson went to his next door neighbors house and called the police. You arrived at about 10:15 P.M. and contacted Mr. Wilson on the sidewalk in front of his home. The house was

38

searched by you for a suspect, but you did not find one. The entire house had been searched by the suspect, and the suspect had thrown clothes and drawers on the floor. The rear door was wide open. Mr. Wilson advised you that he had locked that door as well. You are advised by Mr. Wilson that he left for work at 7:00 AM and all was secure at that time.

You determine the following from your interview of Mr. Wilson:

1. Stolen:
   a. Panasonic TV, 21" screen, Ser #AOK6873461, Model B-2A
   b. Cash, $20.00
2. Business Address: 624 Industrial Way, Anywhere, CA. (510) 686-9710
3. Home Telephone: (510) 970-6577
4. Occupation: Salesman
5. Race: White   Sex: Male   Age: 35   DOB: 9/15/60
6. You can find no witnesses.
7. Mr. Wilson tells you he left home at 5:30 P.M. to go to dinner with his girlfriend.
8. He indicates that he lock all doors on the house.
9. Wilson bought the TV for $275.00. It is two year old.
10. You call the evidence technician to the scene to take fingerprints.
11. Other information: beat *12,* incident *#2567,* case *#XX-226578.*

Note: Some of the appropriate boxes have not been checked. Check them in your textbook, and be prepared to identify them to your instructor.

REPORT 2—UNKNOWN/YOU MUST DECIDE

You are dispatched at 8:40 P.M. to the 7400 Block of MacArthur Blvd in Anywhere, California 95555 on a report of a purse snatch having taken place. When you arrive you contact the victim, a Mrs. Mabel Brown. She is still lying on the sidewalk, being cared for by several citizens. You observe that her knees are skinned up and she has a large gash in her lip. As you talk to her she says that she is OK and does not want to be taken to the hospital in an ambulance.

She tells you the following. At about 8:20 P.M. she was walking back to her house at 2672 76th Ave. She had been at the grocery store. She was carrying her purse in her left hand and her few groceries in her right hand. She heard this car stop behind her but she did not look back. She heard the sound of someone running toward her. She glanced back just in time to see this fist strike her in the mouth. Her purse was snatched from her at the same time. She fell to the sidewalk. She did not see anything after that.

	Beat	Incident number	No. of persons arrested	Case number
Page __1__ *of* __2__ *Pages*	12	2567	0	XX-226578

PERSON 1: ☐ Complainant ☐ Business

Last name	First	Middle initial	Sex	Race	DOB
Wilson	Pete	R.	M	W	9/15/60

Home address	City, State	Zip	Home phone	Work phone
4675 Ascot Drive	Anywhere, CA	95555	(510) 970-6577	(510) 686-9710

Business Address/School	City, State	Zip	Occupation	Work hours
624 Industrial Way	Anywhere, CA	95555	salesman	8:00–5:00

PERSON 2: ☐ Complainant ☐ Business ☐ Reporting person ☐ Witness ☐ Additional comp. listed on pg. ___

Last name	First	Middle initial	Sex	Race	DOB

Home address	City, State	Zip	Home phone	Work phone

Business address/School	City, State	Zip	Occupation	Work hours

CRIME: ☐ Race, ethnic, religious, sexual orientation involved

Common name	Section/Subsection	Code	Date occurred	Time occurred
Burglary	459	PC	4/14/20XX	7:00 AM–9:35 PM

Location (address/block number)		Date reported	Time reported
4675 Ascot Drive, Anywhere, CA 95555		4/14/20XX	10:15 PM

Loss ☐ currency, notes ☐ clothing, furs ☐ jewelry, precious metals ☐ firearms ☐ office equip. ☐ misc.
☐ TVs, radios, stereos ☐ household goods ☐ consumable goods ☐ livestock ☐ motor vehs. ☐ none

WEAPON USED: ☐ Firearm ☐ Cutting/Stabbing instrument ☐ Other ☐ Hands, fist, feet ☐ Foreign object

☐ Assault: complete weapon line   Assault with intent to commit: ☐ rape   ☐ mayhem
☐ Homicide: complete weapon line   ☐ lewd act   ☐ oral copulation

☐ Robbery: type of location   ☐ street   ☐ gas station   ☐ convenience store   ☐ other
☐ bank   ☐ residence   ☐ other commercial

☐ Complete loss and weapon line   ☐ auto   ☐ commercial   Method of entry: ☐ forcible
☐ Burglary: complete loss line   ☐ residential   ☐ other   ☐ unlawful entry, no force   ☐ att. forcible

☐ Theft: complete loss line   ☐ pickpocket   ☐ purse snatch   ☐ auto access.   ☐ auto clout
☐ shoplift   ☐ bicycle   ☐ coin-op device   ☐ other

SUSPECT 1: in custody for offense: ☐ Y ☐ N   Arrest/Citation #: ___   ☐ Additional suspects listed on pg. ___

Last name	First	Middle initial	Sex	Race	DOB	Hgt.	Wgt.	Hair	Eyes

Address/School	City, State	Zip	Home phone	Work phone

Other description (clothes, comlexion, identifying characteristics, words used):

VEHICLE: ☐ Complainant's ☐ Suspect's

License number	State	Year	Make	Model	Body type	Color	Hold placed:	☐ Y	☐ N

Other identifying information: Towed to:

Officer	Serial number	Watch	District	Supervisor	Serial number
J. Vigilant	6948-P	3	III	B. Fairman	7007-P

Generic Crime Report

ADDITIONAL INFORMATION REPORT
ANYWHERE, CA, POLICE DEPARTMENT

	Beat	Incident number	No. of persons arrested	Case number
Page _2_ of _2_ Pages	12	2567	0	XX-226578

PERSON 1: ☐ Complainant ☐ Business

Last name	First	Middle initial	Sex	Race	DOB
Wilson	Pete	R.	M	W	9/15/60

Home address	City, State	Zip	Home phone	Work phone
4675 Ascot Drive	Anywhere, CA	95555	(510) 970-6577	(510) 686-9710

☐ Continuation of: _____   ☐ Offense   ☐ Supplemental   ☐ Arrest
☐ Supplemental report

CRIME:	Common name	Section	Code	Date of original report	Date of this report
	Burglary	459	PC		4/14/20XX

Location		Suspect's name	Sex	Race	DOB
4675 Ascot Drive, Anywhere, CA 95555		unknown			

Vehicle:	License #	State	Year	Make	Model	Color	Operator's license #	State

NARRATIVE:

1. List additional persons, charges, suspects, vehicles.

2. Itemize loss: Give item values and total loss value.

3. Evidence: Itemize, where found, by whom found, disposition

4. Summarize details of incident in logical order.

LOSS:

1. TV, Panasonic, 21" screen, Model B-2A, Serial Number AOK 6873461		$100.00
2. Cash		20.00
	Total =	$120.00

SUMMARY:

On the above date and time of occurence, unknown suspect(s) forcibly entered complaint Wilson's home by breaking the door jamb with an unknown object. After entering the home, the suspect(s) searched every room and threw clothes and drawers on the floors. The suspect(s) took the above described loss and fled out of the rear door, which was found open. There is no other information or leads at this time. Evidence Technician J. Jones (6783-P) was called to take fingerprints but none were found.

Additional Information Report

You are contacted by Mr. Joe Small who tells you he was standing at the bus stop at 75 and MacArthur. He saw the young man who hit Mrs. Brown. Small described him as a light complexion African-American male, about 20–22 years old, 5'10", muscular build, wearing a black baseball cap, an Oakland Raiders jacket and baggy blue jeans. Small tells you that this suspect ran to a waiting vehicle carrying the purse. The vehicle was waiting at the corner of 76th and MacArthur. He tells you that the suspect jumped into the passenger seat of the car and he vehicle sped off southbound on 76th Ave. Small said he got only a very quick look at the driver. He could only describe him as either a young, light complexion, African-American male or Hispanic male.

You are contacted by another witness, Mr. Paul Goodman. He tells you that he was driving directly behind the vehicle that picked up the suspect who snatched the purse. Goodman had his camcorder with him so he stopped well behind the suspect vehicle at 76th and MacArthur. He picked up his camcorder and filmed the suspect vehicle only. He could not remember the vehicle type because he was so busy filming. He tells you that he definitely filmed the license plate and the driver of the vehicle.

Mabel Brown tells you that her purse was a Coach brand leather purse worth aproximately $150.00. In her purse she had exactly $50.00 in cash. Mabel says that she does not own charge cards, and does not drive so she has no driver's license. She says there was some cosmetics in the purse but nothing else of value.

Below is additional information for the report:

Mabel Brown

2672 76th Ave., Anywhere, Ca 95555
(510) 569-1039
Retired postal worker
Female, Black
69, January 12, 1929

Joseph E. Small

5050 Ascot Drive, Anywhere, Ca 95555
Firefighter, Male, Black, 29, November 20, 1966
City of Anywhere Fire Department, Engine #20
(510) 568-3945 h   (510) 273-7400

Paul T. Goodman

23798 Skyline Drive, Anywhere, CA 95555
Securities dealer, Male, White, 46, June 6, 1949
Prudential-Bache Securities, 2400 Market Street,
Everywhere, CA 95566
(510) 589-6620 h   (415) 555-1010

Joe E. Lens

Evidence Technician, Anywhere Police Department, 7191-P, took photos of victim and crime scene

Other information: beat *25*, incident *#5026*, report *#XX-328661*.

REPORT 3—MULTIPLE OFFENSES

You are dispatched to 6820 Hillside Drive at 5:03 A.M. on Tuesday, January 21, 20XX in Anywhere, Ca 95555 on a report of a rape, burglary and automobile theft. When you arrive you are contacted by the victim, Jane Williams, who tells you the following. On the evening before at about 8:30 P.M. she was puting her two children to bed in their bedroom. The children are Melissa Williams, female, white, 9 years and Brad Williams, male, white, 7 years. Jane Williams tells you that she watched TV for about another 1 and $\frac{1}{2}$; hours until 10:00 P.M. Jane emphasized that she was very tired at this point so she went to bed.

Jane said she was awakened at about 11:30 P.M. by a figure standing over her next to her bed. She began to scream, and this man grabed her mouth very hard. He held her mouth shut and held her down. Jane related that this man then stuffed a handkerchief into her mouth. Jane tells you that he had both of his knees on her arms to keep her pinned to the bed.

Jane tells you that he then proceeded to take off his tee-shirt, exposing his chest. It was still dark so Jane could only see a shadow of a figure. It was at this point that the man decided to turn on the lamp on the night table. Now Jane could see the man's face clearly. The man now began to talk to Jane. Jane tells you that this man told her not to struggle and everything would be alright. This man said to Jane, "If you just relax and enjoy it, I won't hurt your children. But if you fight and resist, I'll kill you and your children."

Jane tells you that she was so scared that she just hopped he would rape her and get it over and leave. But that was not what happened. Jane's attacker said, "I want to enjoy this because I don't get a woman very often." Jane said he ripped off her night gown and began fondling her breasts. As he fondled her, the man said, "I'm going to cut you open so I can see the sperm swimming around inside you." Jane said she almost passed out at this point so the man said, "I'm just kidding."

Jane related that he fondled her for over an hour and then took his pants off. He then raped her twice over a period of possibly two hours. When he was finished, he got dressed and removed Jane's handkerchief and asked her where her money was. Jane told him her purse had $75.00 and was in the kitchen.

Jane tells you that he then put the handkerchief back into her mouth and tied her to the bed with rope "by all fours." She could hear the man taking things out of the house for a period of about an hour. Jane said she heard her Jeep Grand Cherokee start up in the garage. She heard the garage door open and her jeep drive out.

At this point, Jane said she began struggling and making as much noise as possible. The time was now 4:45 A.M. Melissa, Jane's daughter, heard her noises and came into her room. She saw her mother's predicament and pulled the handkerchief out of her mouth. Jane then told her to untie the rope. Melissa did so and Jane got up and called 911. That is when you got the call at precisely 4:57 A.M.

Upon your arrival at 5:03 A.M., you talk to Jane, and she relayed the above information to you. You are also contacted by a witness. His name is John Franklin, male, Black, 39, who lives at 6824 Hillside Drive, Anywhere, CA 95555. His telephone number is (510) 888-1111. He works for P.G. & E. as a serviceman, and his work number is (510) 222-5555. He tells you that he waits every morning at the corner of Hillside Drive and 68th Ave. for his ride to work. He said he waits there every morning at 4:30 A.M. for his ride which comes between 4:45–5:00 A.M. This morning he was there at 4:30 A.M. precisely. At about 4:45–4:50 A.M. he saw Jane's garage door open and the jeep drive out hurriedly. He knew this was suspicious because Jane didn't leave for work until 7:30 A.M. He noticed a male white driver which made him even more suspicious because he knew Jane had no boyfriends. He was able to get a good look at the driver because he had the dome light on and was silhouetted nicely against the dark morning. Mr. Franklin tells you he is sure he would be able to recognize the man again.

Your Investigation

Your investigation determines the following:

- The suspect entered the house through Jane's bedroom window. He had managed to pry the window open with a crow bar, which you located and recovered beneath the window.
- There were shoe imprints in the soil beneath the window.
- The suspect removed his wool coat and left it in Jane's room.
- There were semen stains on the sheets.
- Jane had scratched the suspect.
- The bindings had been left on the bed.
- The handkerchief was on the floor next to the bed.
- The following was taken:
  a. TV, Sony, 17", color, portable, serial number ZX2278901
  b. VCR, Sony, Serial number PN32165889
  c. $75.00 cash
  d. Jeep Grand Cherokee, 1996, metallic blue, California license 3AAA111
- Jane described the suspect as: male, white, approximately 35–40, shoulder length sandy blond hair, brown eyes, tattoos as follows: over one nipple "sweet," over the other "sour"; a man beating a woman with a whip. He had a very high pitched voice

and a large scar on the right side of his face. He wore a dirty tank-top type tee shirt and dirty blue jeans. She estimated his height at about 5'10"; he had a muscular build; she estimated that he was about 180–190 pounds. She emphatically stated that she would be able to identify him if she saw either him or a photograph of him.

- Insure that your report includes all of the follow-up activity for which you would be responsible in a rape investigation.
- Evidence Technician, John Poirot, 7228-P, was called to the scene to gather the evidence and take photographs.
- Other information: beat *10,* incident *#6687,* report *#XX-785010.*

REPORT 4—MISSING PERSON

Missing Person Reporting Form

Next you will review the Missing Person Reporting Form. The report form is below, and an abbreviated explanation follows. A scenario follows the form and explanation. After your instructor has covered the form with you, you will take the Missing Person Reporting Form and Additional Information Report from Appendix B and prepare your report. It would be advisable to make copies of the report forms first in case your instructor wants to give you additional missing person scenarios and requires you to prepare additional reports.

Some of the numbered blocks on the sample Missing Person Reporting Form need explanation. In block 4 you see nine choices. The following are the definitions of these nine choices: (1) Runaway Juvenile—missing juvenile that has left home without the knowledge/permission of parents or guardian, (2) Voluntary Missing Adult—missing adult who has left of his/her own free will, (3) Parental/Family Abduction—missing juvenile taken by a parent/non-parental family member, (4) Non-Family Abduction—missing juvenile taken by a known abductor, but not a family member, (5) Stranger Abduction—missing juvenile taken by a stranger or missing under circumstances that may indicate a stranger abduction, (6) Dependent Adult—missing adult who is between the ages of 18 and 64 who has physical or mental limitation which restricts his or her ability to carry out normal activities (i.e., Alzheimer's, mentally handicapped), (7) Lost—any person who has strayed away or whose whereabouts are unknown, (8) Catastrophe—any person who is missing after a catastrophe (i.e., plane crash, boating accident, fire, flood), and (9) Unknown Circumstances—when circumstances surrounding the missing person's disappearance are unknown.

In block 7 you see three choices. Check all that apply. *At Risk* includes, but is not limited to, evidence or indications the missing person is/has: (1) the victim of a crime or foul play, (2) in need of medical attention, (3) no pattern of running away or disappearing,

MISSING PERSON REPORTING FORM

1. Check one: ☐ ADULT ☐ JUVENILE

2. Reporting Agency _____

3. Case # _____

5. Department of Justice # _____ 6. NCIC # _____

7. Category: ☐ At Risk ☐ Prior Missing ☐ Sexual Exploitation Suspected

8. Name _____ Date/Time Missing _____

9. Alias 1 _____ Alias 2 _____

4. RECORD TYPE
(Check type best describes)

☐ Runaway Juvenile
☐ Voluntary Missing Adult
☐ Parental/Family Abduction
☐ Non-Family Abduction
☐ Stranger Abduction
☐ Dependent Adult
☐ Lost
☐ Catastrophe
☐ Unknown Circumstances

10. Gender	11. Race	12. Hgt.	13. Wgt.	14. Eye Color	15. Hair Color/Length	16. DOB
☐ Male	☐ W ☐ J ☐ H ☐ F			☐ Blk ☐ Haz ☐ Blu ☐ Mar	☐ Blk ☐ Red ☐ Bln ☐ Sdy	
☐ Female	☐ B ☐ O ☐ I ☐ X			☐ Bro ☐ Pnk ☐ Gry ☐ Mul	☐ Bro ☐ Wht ☐ Gry ☐ XXX	
☐ Unknown	☐ C			☐ Grn ☐ XXX	Length _____	

17. Residence Address _____ City, State _____

18. Location Last Seen _____ Probable Destination _____

19. Known Associates _____

20. Mental Condition _____

21. SS # _____ FBI # _____ DL # _____

22. Photo Available? ☐ yes ☐ no   Age in Photo _____

   Photo/X-ray Waiver Release Signed? ☐ yes ☐ no   (Attach photo and signed waiver release form.)

23. Scars/Marks/Tattoos (Locate/Describe) _____

24. Skeletal X-rays Available? ☐ yes ☐ no   Broken Bones/Missing Organs _____

25. Dental X-rays Available? ☐ yes ☐ no   (Attach chart and X-rays.)

   Dentures: ☐ Upper ☐ Lower ☐ Full ☐ Partial

26. Visible Dental Work _____

27. Dentist's Name _____ Phone _____

28. Glasses ☐ Contact Lenses ☐ Clothing Description/Size _____

29. Jewelry Description _____

30. If Vehicle Involved: ☐ S ☐ MP   Lic # _____ Make _____ Model _____ Yr _____

31. If abduction, did abduction involve movement of missing person in the commission of a crime? yes ☐ no ☐

32. Suspect's Name _____ DOB _____

33. Relationship to Victim _____

34. Reporting Party _____ Phone _____

35. Relationship to Missing Person _____ Date Reported _____

36. Additional Information _____

37. Reporting Officer/Agency _____ Phone _____

Missing Person Reporting Form

(4) the victim of a parental abduction, and (5) mentally impaired. *Prior Missing* indicates the missing person has been previously reported as missing. *Sexual Exploitation Suspected* means just that—the reporting party suspects the missing person may be sexually exploited/abused.

In block 11 the letters translate as follows: *W-White, H-Hispanic, B-Black, I-American Indian, C-Chinese, J-Japanese, F-Filipino, O-all other, X-unknown.* In block 14, MUL is Multi-color and XXX is unknown. In block 20 *Mental Condition* refers to the missing person's state of mind: stable, suicidal, depressed, etc.

Block 22 reminds the officer to obtain a photo of the missing person that is as recent as possible. Most agencies require the reporting officer to get a signed waiver on a separate form when taking a photo or X-rays. Complete block 30 if there is a known vehicle involved; check *S* if it is the suspect's vehicle or *MP* if it is the missing person's vehicle. This should explain how to use the missing person report. Now you will be given a scenario of a missing person incident. Use the Missing Person Reporting Form and the Continuation Report in Appendix B to complete your report.

Missing Person Case

On Tuesday, March 12, 2002 at 1835 hours, you are dispatched to 2920 Wildwood Way, Anywhere, California 95555 on a report of a missing 3-year-old boy. You contact Mrs. Pat Bryant who indicates she is the boy's mother. She tells you the boy's name is Zachary Bryant, DOB January 12, 1999. Mrs. Bryant is very hysterical. She says that she has searched the imediate area and talked to all of her neighbors but no one has seen Zachary.

Mrs. Bryant tells you that she last saw Zachary at about 1750 hours in the backyard riding on his plastic "Hot Wheel" tricycle. She indicates that she found the gate leading from the backyard to the front yard open and that it does not latch properly. She believes that Zachary must have pushed the door open with his "Hot Wheel" and ridden off somewhere in the neighborhood. Mrs. Bryant tells you that Zachary does not know his exact address or his telephone number so he could not give this information to anyone who might determine he is lost. You tell her that someone will probably determine he is lost and call the Anywhere Police Department with the information and officers will be able to go to this location, pick him up, and take him home. Mrs. Bryant asks you what will happen if a stranger or pedophile finds him and does not call the Anywhere Police Department. You assure her that officers will be searching for him every minute until he is found. You tell her that officers are already in the area looking for him.

Mrs. Bryant tells you that Zachary has never done this before, but she believes he could pedal the "Hot Wheel" for quite some distance, if he stayed on the sidewalks. She believes he would have stopped to play with any other children his age.

You obtain a photo of Zachary, which was taken on his 3rd birthday, and have Mrs. Bryant sign the waiver form. Your investigation results in the following information:

- Zachary J. Bryant, DOB 01/12/99, White male, 33 inches tall, 56 pounds, brown eyes, blond hair, wearing blue corduroy pants, blue sneakers, and a yellow and pink zip-up jacket with a soccer player kicking a soccer ball on the front. The "Hot Wheel" is yellow and red plastic with large black rear wheels and one very large front wheel with foot pedals. The "Hot Wheel" is in the "chopped" style and has blue and yellow streamers coming out of the plastic handle bar grips.
- Case #02-195776
- Zachary's SSN—000-01-0000

Prepare your report using the forms in Appendix B.

REPORT 5—INCIDENT REPORT

The final type of report that you will learn about is the incident report. Incident reports are used by law enforcement agencies to document noncriminal complaints so that there is a record of the officer's time and disposition of the service call. Examples of these sorts of calls are barking dog complaints, minor disputes where neither party wishes to make a formal complaint, and civil cases when the officer has no probable cause to arrest and the agency has no jurisdiction. An example of a civil call often faced by law enforcement officers is when the calling party has lent money to someone who has not paid it back and the calling party wants the officer to force the person to pay back the loan. Another frequent situation is when a landlord has not been paid the rent on the agreed date and he wants the officers to force the tenants to pay or tell them to get out.

Incident Report Case

Using the following information and the Incident Report form in Appendix B, complete your report. On April 25, 2002 at 0110 hours you are dispatched to 1010 Merle Ave. on the report of a barking dog. You contact Mrs. Beatrice Campbell who tells you that her neighbor's dog has been barking loudly for 2 hours and she cannot sleep. Her home telephone number is 666-6666. The incident number is 02-25-0011. Prepare your incident report.

DESCRIPTIONS IN YOUR REPORTS

Descriptions of Jewelry

Ring, diamond, 1 karat, marquise-shaped, gold band, size 6
Ring, ruby, baguette-shaped, platinum band, size 10
Necklace, 35 pearls, size 16 inches

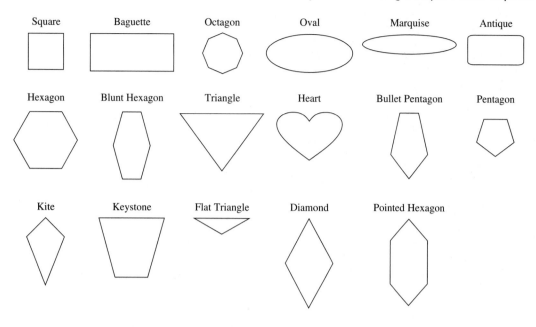

Standard Shapes of Precious Stones

> Note: It is often best to actually try to draw a picture of the jewelry item on your report. Jewelry items can be very unique in their design. Many people like to have jewelers design jewelry for them in a specific fashion.

Descriptions of Commonly Stolen or Burglarized Property

Firearms

- Revolver, Colt, 38 Special #52685, Serial #7891011, No Owner Applied #, 4" barrel, blue finish, walnut grips
- Pistol (semi-automatic), Glock, 9mm, Model 17, Serial #45678, No Owner Applied #, 4" barrel, stainless steel, stock grips

Appliances

- TV, Sony, Model VH-2, Serial #S-123-Q-456, Owner Applied #086-42-6789, 28", color, chrome face, black exterior
- Vacuum cleaner, Hoover, Model 10-HVC (Wind Tunnel), serial #VC-286-65-I, Owner Applied #555-55-5555, upright, green exterior

Electronics

- Video recorder, Panasonic, Model XK3, serial #123456, Owner Applied #619-61-6191, 4-head, black head, chrome face
- Camera-recorder, Sony, Model PX2381, serial #234567, No Owner Applied #, black exterior

Money

- Cash, 10 x $20.00 bills ($200), 5 x $100.00 bills ($500) = $700.00
- Checks, Bank of the West, Personalized—John P. Jones, account #134077634, checks #1141–1175

Descriptions of Suspects, Clothing, and Vehicles

Suspects, Clothing, and Vehicles

Sex: Male, Female, Transvestite

Race/Ethnicity: Black, Caucasian, Hispanic, Oriental, Indian, Other

Age: Under 15, 15–17, 18–20, Early or Late 20s, 30s, 40s, 50s, 60s

Height: Under 5'0", 5'0', 5'2", 5'4", 5'6", 5'8", 5'10", 6'0", 6'2", etc.

Weight: Under 100 lbs., 100 lbs., 120 lbs., 140 lbs., 160 lbs., 180 lbs., 200 lbs., 220 lbs., 240 lbs., etc.

Build: Thin, Slim, Medium Average, Heavy, Husky, Muscular, Fat

Hair:
    Color—Black, Brown, Blond, Dirty Blond, Red, Gray, White
    Style—Straight, Curly, Wavy, Afro, Tied, Neat, Wig
    Length—Crew Cut, Neck, Shoulder, Long

Eyes: Black, Brown, Blue, Green, Hazel, Gray

Glasses: Sunglasses, Prescription, Wire Frame, Plastic Frame, Rimless
    Frames—Clear, Brown, Black, Gold, Silver, Other

Complexion: Pale, Fair, Medium, Ruddy, Tanned, Brown, Black, Clear, Acne, Pock-Marked

Facial Hair: Mustache, Beard, Goatee
    Color—Black, Brown, Blond, Red, Gray, White

Peculiarities: Walk, Mannerisms, Speech, Accent, Tattoos, Scars, Injuries, Jewelry, Other

Hat: Baseball Cap, Knit Cap, Other
    Color—Blue, Red, etc.
    Design—Patches, Feathers, Ornamentation

Shirt/Blouse: Pullover, T-shirt, Sport Shirt, Dress Shirt, Tank Top, Other
    Sleeve Length—Short, Long, Sleeveless
    Color

Trousers/Slacks: Jeans, Shorts, Dress Slacks, Sport Slacks, Knit Pants, Corduroy
    Color

Shoes: Barefoot, Slippers, Dress Shoes, Work Shoes, Boots, Sandals

Dress: Short, Long
    Color

Vehicle: Car, Van, Small Pickup, Truck, Motorcycle, Moped, Bicycle

Make—AMC, Buick, Chevrolet, Chrysler, Datsun, Dodge, Ford, Mercury, Oldsmobile, Plymouth, Pontiac, Toyota, Volkswagen, Other
Color
Type—2-Dr., 4-Dr., Station Wagon, Hatchback
License _____ State _____
Other
I.D.—Description: Rust, Tires, Upholstery, Sunroof, Other

Descriptions of Injuries

You should not try to be too specific about injuries. If you write in your report, for example, that the victim sustained shotgun wounds to the abdomen because you see several entry wounds, it may turn out that these were multiple wounds from a handgun. The public defender or defense attorney will surely make you look foolish during direct examination, and the jury may question your expertise in this and other areas as a result (refer to Chapter 16 for specifics). Therefore, be very general in your descriptions. By saying "gunshot wounds," you include shotgun, handgun, rifle, etc., because these are all guns. Some examples of proper descriptions of injuries include:

- The victim sustained gunshot wounds to the chest (abdomen, shoulder, etc.).
- The victim sustained stab wounds to the abdomen (back, etc.).
- The victim sustained slash wounds to the face (neck, back, etc.).
- The victim sustained blunt instrument trauma wounds to the head (shoulders, etc.).
- The victim sustained bludgeon wounds to the head from a large striking instrument such as a bat (tire iron, etc.). When the wounds to the head show that the skull was crushed, you can be vague in your description of the actual instrument by using the phrase "such as a . . ." You can also write, "The victim's skull was crushed in the rear (side, front)."

Descriptions of Property Damage

Property damage can encompass a great number of areas. However, most often included in property damage are vehicle damage as a result of an accident, hit-and-run, vandalism, and out-of-control or drunk drivers who drive over a lawn or into a fence, fire hydrant, telephone pole, street sign, home, or business. There is really no set format for writing descriptions of property damage. An example might be as follows: "Extensive damage to fire hydrant number 231 (or at the NW corner of Main and Poplar Streets), which was broken off, causing water to flood the 3600 Block of Main Street." The best way to describe property damage is to look at the situation and make sure that you have included everything you saw that was damaged and describe it in some logical sequence. As with jewelry, another good approach is to draw a diagram or picture of the damage on your report. Drawing templates is the best tool you can employ for this purpose.

5

Writing Sample Correctional Reports

In Chapter 5 you will actually write two correctional officer reports, as if you were actually working as a correctional officer and these incidents happened on your shift. You will play two roles. You will be the actual reporting correctional officer for the incident that happens, and you will be the lieutenant in charge of that facility who prepares the follow-up report to be sent to the State Department of Corrections headquarters. Before writing the two reports, however, you will be given a sample report, which your instructor will review with you in detail so that you know exactly how to complete the reports you are given. *Use the sample blank forms provided in* Appendix B *for your reports.*

Before you begin this part of the lesson, I will cover the standard policies that govern the preparation of reports and the submission of these reports to the state headquarters. The following procedure defines staff responsibility and provides procedures and criteria for reporting incidents occurring within the State Department of Corrections.

REPORTABLE INCIDENTS AND REPORT FORMS

The following are examples of incidents that correctional staff are required to report and submit to State Department of Corrections headquarters:

- Felonies committed by inmates, parolees, employees, or the public on institution property, during transportation, or under the jurisdiction of parole regions
- General or partial lockdowns
- Riots, inmate strikes, or general demonstrations
- Major power failures
- Serious accidents or injuries
- Deaths
- Significant damage or destruction of state property
- Escapes or attempted escapes

- Any state of emergency as defined in the Code of Regulations
- Any use or discharge of weapons, chemical agents, or tasers
- Threats against the President or Vice President of the United States, or threats against state officials
- Safety grievances of employees
- Employee job actions

Written reports to the state headquarters will be reported on Form 840, which is enclosed in Appendix B and which you will use to make your state headquarters reports. Form 840 has three parts: A, B and C. Form 840-A is the Cover Sheet, Form 840-B is the Involved Parties, and Form 840-C is the Supplemental. The other forms you will be using to write your sample reports are Form 839, Supplement to Crime/Incident Report, and Form 839-A, Supplement to Crime/Incident Report. The latter two forms are used by the actual reporting correctional officer to report the incident he witnessed or assisted; the facility lieutenant uses these reports to prepare the state report on Forms 840 A, B, and C. There is one other form you will use in preparing your reports. It is the Medical Report of Injury or Unusual Occurrence. This form, along with the others listed above, will be provided for you in Appendix B to copy for your reports.

The sample report you will review in class refers to other reports with which you should be familiar, *but which you will not use for your reports*. One is the Rules Violation Report (Form 118), which goes into the inmate's file and can be used as the basis for a disciplinary hearing. Another is the Victim's Chrono (Form 119), which gives a short description of the victim inmate's enemies as a result of an assault. Two other forms that correctional officers commonly use, but which are not included in the Appendix, are the Use of Force Report and the Use of Firearms Report. Another form that is not used as frequently is the Workman's Compensation Form, which would be completed by a correctional officer who was injured in the line of duty and who required a medical leave of absence. So, as you can see, there are many forms and much paperwork required for the position of correctional officer. It is important that you follow the instructor's review of the sample report so that you can put your best effort into writing your two reports and be that much closer to becoming a good report writing correctional officer.

SAMPLE REPORT

On pages 55–70, you and the instructor will review the sample correctional reports. There are *built-in errors* in the reports. In particular, many of the appropriate boxes are not checked. You should edit the report for these built-in errors, using the editing symbols you learned in Chapter 3 and checking the appropriate boxes. Be prepared to discuss these with your instructor. In addition, you should begin to get a good idea of how to prepare the correctional report, and this sample report will serve as your guide when you write the two reports included in this book.

STATE PRISON USA
CRIME/INCIDENT REPORT
PART A—COVER SHEET

Incident Log Number
STA-04B-98-5910

FORM 840-A

Institution/Facility	Incident Site/Location	Date Occurred	Time Occurred
State Prison USA	**4B2R/SHU, Exercise Yard #2**	**10/22/03**	**0855**

Specific Crime/Incident	D.A. Referral	Section/Code/Rule number
Battery on an Inmate Resulting in S.B.I.	☐ Yes ☐ No	**3005 c Force and Violence**

N SERT Activated? Y or N	**N** Negotiation Team Activated? Y or N	**N** Mutual Aid Requested? Y or N	**N** Media Notified? Y or N

Related Information (Check All That Apply)

Deaths	Cause of Death	Assault/Battery	Type of Assault/Battery	
☐ Staff	☐ Homicide	☐ On staff	☐ Beating	☐ Strangling
☐ Visitor	☐ Suicide	☐ On visitor	☐ Shooting	☐ Slashing
☐ Inmate	☐ Accidental	☐ On inmate	☐ Stabbing	☐ Sexual
☐ N/A	☐ Natural	☐ Other _____	☐ Spearing	☐ Other _____
	☐ N/A		☐ Poisoning	

Serious Injury	Inmate Weapons		Shots Fired	Type Weapon (Staff)
☐ Staff	☐ Firearm	☐ Stabbing instrument	☐ Yes ☐ No	☐ 38-Cal.
☐ Visitor	☐ Knife	☐ Hands/Feet		☐ Mini-14
☐ Inmate	☐ Spear	☐ Club/Bludgeon	Number	☐ H&K .94
☐ Accidental	☐ Explosive	☐ Caustic substance	Fired ___2___	☐ Shotgun
☐ Attempted	☐ Projectile	☐ Other _____	Escapes	
suicide	☐ Slashing instrument	☐ Inmate		
☐ Other _____	☐ Commercial	manufactured	☐ With Force	☐ 37-mm
		☐ N/A	☐ Without force	☐ Taser
			☐ Attempted	☐ PR-24
				☐ Other _____

Suspected Controlled Substance	Lockdowns	Exceptional Activity	
☐ Heroin/Opiates	☐ Yes ☐ No	☐ Major disturbance	☐ Employee job action
☐ Cocaine	If yes, list affected	☐ Inmate strike	☐ Major power outage
☐ Marijunana	programs below:	☐ Public demonstration	☐ Explosion
☐ Amphetamine		☐ Inmate demonstration	☐ Fire
☐ Barbiturate		☐ Natural disaster	☐ Hostage
☐ LSD		☐ Environmental hazard	☐ Gang involved
☐ PCP		☐ "Special interest inmate"	☐ Other _____
☐ Methamphetamine		☐ Weather	
☐ Other _____		☐ N/A	
☐ N/A			

Description of Crime/Incident:

On Thursday, October 22, 2003, at approximately 0855 hours, an act of Battery on an Inmate Resulting in Serious Bodily Injury occurred in Facility 4B2R/SHU, Exercise Yard #2, Yard Group "B-1" Controlled, involving Inmates Brown, K-25791, 4B2R-04L; White, K-52489, 4B2R-07R; and Black, J-89660, 4B2R-18L.

Correctional Officer P. Thomas, assigned as the 4B2R Exercise Yard Gunner, observed Inmate Black enter the yard and approach Inmate White. After a brief discussion, Inmates White and Black approached Inmate Brown and simultaneously began striking him with clenched fists to the head and upper torso area, knocking Inmate Brown to the ground. Officer Thomas activated the unit alarm and immediately began giving verbal commands to "stop fighting" and "get down," with negative results.

☐ Check here if description is continued on Part C.

Name/Title/Signature of Reporting Staff	Badge/I.D. #	Service (Institution Use)	Date
I. M. Incharge, Correctional Lieutenant, IV-B	**34628**	**17** years **11** months	**10/23/03**

Authorized Signature/Title (Institution Use)			
I. B. Mean, Correctional Facility Captain			**10/23/03**

Crime/Incident Report

STATE PRISON USA
CRIME/INCIDENT REPORT
PART C—SUPPLEMENTAL

Page __2__ of __7__ Pages

Incident Log Number
STA-04B-98-5910

FORM 840-C

Institution/Facility	Date Occurred	Time Occurred
State Prison USA, 4B2R/SHU, Exercise Yard #2	**10/22/03**	**0855**

Type of Information

☐ Continuing description of incident (Part A)   ☐ Supplemental information   ☐ Closure report

Narrative:

    Due to the threat of serious injury occurring, Officer Thomas discharged one (1) #264W multiple baton round from the assigned 37mm launcher, serial # D-13445. The wooden blocks ricocheted approximately nine (9) feet in front of the combatants, with negative results. Inmates White and Black continued their assault on Inmate Brown, as he lay in a fetal position with both arms covering his head, trying to protect himself. Officer Thomas discharged one (1) additional #264W round, ricocheting the blocks approximately nine (9) feet in from of the combatants, again with negative results. Inmate Brown was now lying on his right side in a limp fashion, apparently unable to protect himself as Inmate White began kicking him in the head. Upon seeing Brown's apparent unconscious state, Officer Thomas drew his state-issue Ruler Mini-14, serial # 18660030 from its assigned gun rack, stating a warning, "Stop fighting; I have the Mini," with positive results, as all inmates assumed prone positions on the ground.

    Correctional Sergeants E. Zedillo and A. Vogelsman responded to the alarm with Medical Technical Assistants I. M. Helpful and F. A. Kit. Inmate White and Black were placed into mechanical restraints (handcuffs) and escorted to separate holding cells where they were medically examined and cleared by MTA Kit. Inmate White sustained no injuries. Inmate Black received abrasions to the left ankle and right shoulder. The abrasions to Inmate Black's right shoulder is consistent with being caused by a discharged wooden block. Inmates White and Black were re-housed wihout further incident.

    Due to Inmate Brown's injuries and inability to safety exit the yard on his own, he was assisted by Sergeants Zedillo and Vogelsman and Correctional Officers B. Womack, T. Munoz, and C. Groeneveld. Inmate Brown was placed on a stokes litter and carried to the rotunda where he was medically examined by MTA Kit, who referred him to State Prison #2's Acute Care Hospital (ACH). Inmate Brown received contusions to the left and right side head and lips, bruises to the right eye, nose, and left cheek, and abrasions to the left hand and nose. At the ACH, Inmate Brown was treated and cleared by Medical Doctor I. R. Scope, who noted that Inmate Brown had sustained a concussion. Inmate Brown was subsequently returned to the facility and re-housed in another building without incident. No staff or other inmates received injuries as a result of this incident or the discharged 37mm launcher. The prognosis for full recovery of the injured inmates is good.

    Because of Inmate Brown's injuries, the State Prison #2 Investigative Services Unit was contacted and responded to 4B2R. The 4B2R Yard #2 was searched for weapons and contraband, with negative results. ISU Correctional Officer S. Holmes took photographs of the inmates and the crime scene, submitting them to the Level-IV Evidence Room, Locker #4. Officers Munoz and Womack collected evidence from the involved inmates, which they submitted to the Level-IV Evidence Room, Locker #5. All ten (10) discharged wooden blocks were recovered and disposed of per institutional procedures. The yard video was secured at the IV-B Captain's Office for administrative review.

Name/Title/Signature of Reporting Staff	Badge/I.D. #	Service (Institution Use)	Date
I. M. Incharge, Correctional Lieutenant, IV-B	**34628**	**17** years **11** months	**10/23/03**

Authorized Signature/Title (Institution Use)			
I. B. Mean, Correctional Facility Captain			**10/23/03**

Crime/Incident Report (*Continued*)

Incident Log Number
STA-04B-98-5910

FORM 840-C

Institution/Facility	Date Occurred	Time Occurred
State Prison USA 4B2R/SHU, Exercise Yard #2	**10/22/03**	**0855**

Type of Information

☐ Continuing description of incident (Part A)   ☐ Supplemental information   ☐ Closure report

Narrative:

Sergeant Zedillo prepared a Victim's Chrono and issued it to Inmate Brown substantiating him as the victim of a Battery on an Inmate Resulting in Serious Bodily Injury.

Sergeant Zedillo also prepared Rules Violation Reports (Form 125), log numbers 4B-98-10-036 and 4B-98-10-037, charging Inmates White and Black, respectively, with violating the Rules and Regulations of the Department of Corrections, Section 3005 ©, Force and Violence, for the specific act of Battery on an Inmate Resulting in Serious Bodily Injury. These Rules Violation Reports will be processed in accordance with institutional procedures.

This incident will be referred to the county District Attorney's Office for felony prosecution if deemed appropriate after review by the investigative lieutenant. If this incident is deemed appropriate for prosecution, Inmates White and Black will be informed of their constitutional rights by the State Prison #2 Investigative Services Unit (ISU). All appropriate administrative staff and the institutional investigator were informed of this incident; the news media were not. All procedural requirements have been met.

I shall keep you (state corrections headquarters) informed of further developments in this matter by Supplemental Report(s).

Name/Title/Signature of Reporting Staff	Badge/I.D. #	Service (Institution Use)	Date
I. M. Incharge, Correctional Lieutenant, IV-B	**34628**	**17** years **11** months	**10/23/03**

Authorized Signature/Title (Institution Use)			
I. B. Mean, Correctional Facility Captain			**10/23/03**

Crime/Incident Report (*Continued*)

FORM 840-B   *Page* __4__ *of* __7__ *Pages*

Institution/Facility	Date Occurred	Time Occurred	Incident Log Number
State Prison USA, 4B2R/SHU, Exercise Yard 2	**10/22/03**	**0855**	**STA-04B-98-5910**

Inmates

Name (Last, First, MI)	Sex	Ethnicity	Class Score
Brown, C.	**M**	**Black**	**56**

Check one	Inmate Number	CII #	FBI #	SS #	PV. RTC?
☐ Victim	**K-25791**	**A-70170826**	**698046SAI**	**XXX-XX-2385**	**Yes**
☐ Suspect	Date Received by	Date Received by	Anticipated Release	Date of Birth	Housing Assignment
☐ Witness	Prison **10/8/01**	State **7/11/00**	Date **11/4/03**	**7/12/73**	**4B2R-04L**

Commitment Offenses (Optional)	County of Commitment
Possession and Purchase of Cocaine for Sale	**San Jacinto**

Description of Injuries **Contusion left & right to head and lips; bruises to right eye and nose**	Prison Gang/Disruptive Group (Validated) **N/A**

Check All That Apply				Location of Hospital/Treatment
☐ Hospitalized	☐ Treated and Released	☐ Refused Treatment	☐ Deceased	**4B2R Rotunda and ACH**

Name (Last, First, MI)	Sex	Ethnicity	Class Score
White, I.	**M**	**Black**	**52**

Check One	Inmate Number	CII #	FBI #	SS #	PV. RTC?
☐ Victim	**K-52489**	**A0976094**	**115037ABO**	**XXX-XX-8985**	**No**
☐ Suspect	Date Received by	Date Received by	Anticipated Release	Date of Birth	Housing Assignment
☐ Witness	Prison **7/31/01**	State **12/4/00**	Date **6/30/2004**	**3/13/76**	**4B2R-07R**

Commitment Offenses (Optional)	County of Commitment
Attempted Murder	**Los Feliz**

Description of Injuries **N/A**	Prison Gang/Disruptive Group (Validated) **N/A**

Check All That Apply				Location of Hospital/Treatment
☐ Hospitalized	☐ Treated and Released	☐ Refused Treatment	☐ Deceased	**4B2R Holding Cell**

Staff, Visitors, Others

Name (Last, First, MI)	Title	Sex	Ethnicity	Regular Days Off
Thomas, P.	**Correctional Officer**	**M**	**White**	**F/S**

Check One	Check One	Badge/I.D. #	Post Assignment	I.D. #
☐ Victim	☐ Staff	**35135**	**4B2R Yard Gunner**	**P122285**
☐ Suspect	☐ Visitor	Description of Injuries		
☐ Witness	☐ Other _____	**N/A**		

Check All That Apply **N/A**				Location of Hospital/Treatment
☐ Hospitalized	☐ Treated and Released	☐ Refused Treatment	☐ Deceased	**N/A**

Name (Last, First, MI)	Title	Sex	Ethnicity	Regular Days Off
Zedillo, E.	**Correctional Sgt.**	**M**	**Hispanic**	**S/M**

Check One	Check One	Badge/I.D. #	Post Assignment	I.D. #
☐ Victim	☐ Staff	**26213**	**4B2R Fac. Sgt. #1**	**P95823**
☐ Suspect	☐ Visitor	Description of Injuries		
☐ Witness	☐ Other _____	**N/A**		

Check All That Apply **N/A**				Location of Hospital/Treatment
☐ Hospitalized	☐ Treated and Released	☐ Refused Treatment	☐ Deceased	**N/A**

Name (Last, First, MI)	Title	Sex	Ethnicity	Regular Days Off
Incharge, I. M.	**Correctional Lt.**	**M**	**White**	**S/S**

Check One	Check One	Badge/I.D. #	Post Assignment	I.D. #
☐ Victim	☐ Staff	**33522**	**4B Facility Lieutenant**	**P100719**
☐ Suspect	☐ Visitor	Description of Injuries		
☐ Witness	☐ Other _____	**N/A**		

Check All That Apply **N/A**				Location of Hospital/Treatment
☐ Hospitalized	☐ Treated and Released	☐ Refused Treatment	☐ Deceased	**N/A**

Crime/Incident Report (*Continued*)

FORM 840-B

Page __5__ of __7__ **Pages**

Institution/Facility	Date Occurred	Time Occurred	Incident Log Number
State Prison USA	**10/22/03**	**0855**	**STA-04B-98-5910**

Inmates

Name (Last, First, MI)				Sex	Ethnicity	Class Score
Black, P.				**M**	**Black**	**103**

Check one	Inmate Number	CII #	FBI #	SS #	PV. RTC?
☐ Victim	**J-89660**	**A-10759097**	**4726851CB0**	**XXX-XX-5196**	**Yes**
☐ Suspect ☐ Witness	Date Received by Prison **9/30/03**	Date Received by State **5/4/02**	Anticipated Release Date **4/13/2033**	Date of Birth **2/2/79**	Housing Assignment **4B2R-07R**

Commitment Offenses (Optional)	County of Commitment
Murder	**Citrus**

Description of Injuries **Abrasions to left ankle & right shoulder** **(block hit)**	Prison Gang/Disruptive Group (Validated) **N/A**

Check All That Apply	Location of Hospital/Treatment
☐ Hospitalized ☐ Treated and Released ☐ Refused Treatment ☐ Deceased	**4B2R Holding Cell**

Name (Last, First, MI)				Sex	Ethnicity	Class Score

Check One	Inmate Number	CII #	FBI #	SS #	PV. RTC?
☐ Victim					
☐ Suspect ☐ Witness	Date Received by Prison	Date Received by State	Anticipated Release Date	Date of Birth	Housing Assignment

Commitment Offenses (Optional)	County of Commitment

Description of Injuries	Prison Gang/Disruptive Group (Validated)

Check All That Apply	Location of Hospital/Treatment
☐ Hospitalized ☐ Treated and Released ☐ Refused Treatment ☐ Deceased	

Staff, Visitors, Others

Name (Last, First, MI)		Title	Sex	Ethnicity	Regular Days Off
Vogelsman, A.		**Correctional Sgt.**	**M**	**White**	**F/S**

Check One	Check One	Badge/I.D. #	Post Assignment	I.D. #
☐ Victim	☐ Staff	**35883**	**4B Fac. Sgt. #2**	**P15745**
☐ Suspect ☐ Witness	☐ Visitor ☐ Other _____	Description of Injuries **N/A**		

Check All That Apply **N/A**	Location of Hospital/Treatment
☐ Hospitalized ☐ Treated and Released ☐ Refused Treatment ☐ Deceased	**N/A**

Name (Last, First, MI)		Title	Sex	Ethnicity	Regular Days Off
Munoz, T.		**Correctional Off.**	**M**	**Hispanic**	**S/M**

Check One	Check One	Badge/I.D. #	Post Assignment	I.D. #
☐ Victim	☐ Staff	**35023**	**4B2L #3**	**P15811**
☐ Suspect ☐ Witness	☐ Visitor ☐ Other _____	Description of Injuries **N/A**		

Check All That Apply **N/A**	Location of Hospital/Treatment
☐ Hospitalized ☐ Treated and Released ☐ Refused Treatment ☐ Deceased	**N/A**

Name (Last, First, MI)		Title	Sex	Ethnicity	Regular Days Off
Womack, B.		**Correctional Off.**	**M**	**White**	**F/S**

Check One	Check One	Badge/I.D. #	Post Assignment	I.D. #
☐ Victim	☐ Staff	**36148**	**4B2R #3**	**P93866**
☐ Suspect ☐ Witness	☐ Visitor ☐ Other _____	Description of Injuries **N/A**		

Check All That Apply **N/A**	Location of Hospital/Treatment
☐ Hospitalized ☐ Treated and Released ☐ Refused Treatment ☐ Deceased	**N/A**

Crime/Incident Report (*Continued*)

Institution/Facility	Date Occurred	Time Occurred	Incident Log Number
State Prison USA, 4B2R/SHU, Exercise Yard #2	**10/22/03**	**0855**	**STA-04B-98-5910**

Inmates

Name (Last, First, MI)				Sex	Ethnicity	Class Score
N/A						

Check one	Inmate Number	CII #	FBI #	SS #		PV. RTC?
☐ Victim						
☐ Suspect	Date Received by Prison	Date Received by State	Anticipated Release Date	Date of Birth	Housing Assignment	
☐ Witness						

Commitment Offenses (Optional)	County of Commitment

Description of Injuries	Prison Gang/Disruptive Group (Validated)

Check All That Apply

☐ Hospitalized   ☐ Treated and Released   ☐ Refused Treatment   ☐ Deceased

Location of Hospital/Treatment

Name (Last, First, MI)				Sex	Ethnicity	Class Score
N/A						

Check One	Inmate Number	CII #	FBI #	SS #		PV. RTC?
☐ Victim						
☐ Suspect	Date Received by Prison	Date Received by State	Anticipated Release Date	Date of Birth	Housing Assignment	
☐ Witness						

Commitment Offenses (Optional)	County of Commitment

Description of Injuries	Prison Gang/Disruptive Group (Validated)

Check All That Apply

☐ Hospitalized   ☐ Treated and Released   ☐ Refused Treatment   ☐ Deceased

Location of Hospital/Treatment

Staff, Visitors, Others

Name (Last, First, MI)	Title	Sex	Ethnicity	Regular Days Off
Helpful, I. M.	**MTA**	**F**	**White**	**S/M**

Check One	Check One	Badge/I.D. #	Post Assignment	I.D. #
☐ Victim	☐ Staff	**41127**	**4B Med. Clinic**	**P93753**
☐ Suspect	☐ Visitor	Description of Injuries		
☐ Witness	☐ Other_____	**N/A**		

Check All That Apply   **N/A**   Location of Hospital/Treatment

☐ Hospitalized   ☐ Treated and Released   ☐ Refused Treatment   ☐ Deceased   **N/A**

Name (Last, First, MI)	Title	Sex	Ethnicity	Regular Days Off
Kit, F. A.	**MTA**	**M**	**White**	**M/T**

Check One	Check One	Badge/I.D. #	Post Assignment	I.D. #
☐ Victim	☐ Staff	**58007**	**4B Med. Clinic**	**P26031**
☐ Suspect	☐ Visitor	Description of Injuries		
☐ Witness	☐ Other_____	**N/A**		

Check All That Apply   **N/A**   Location of Hospital/Treatment

☐ Hospitalized   ☐ Treated and Released   ☐ Refused Treatment   ☐ Deceased   **N/A**

Name (Last, First, MI)	Title	Sex	Ethnicity	Regular Days Off
Groeneveld, C.	**Correctional Off.**	**M**	**White**	**T/W**

Check One	Check One	Badge/I.D. #	Post Assignment	I.D. #
☐ Victim	☐ Staff	**56743**	**4B2R #3**	**P26130**
☐ Suspect	☐ Visitor	Description of Injuries		
☐ Witness	☐ Other_____	**N/A**		

Check All That Apply   **N/A**   Location of Hospital/Treatment

☐ Hospitalized   ☐ Treated and Released   ☐ Refused Treatment   ☐ Deceased   **N/A**

Crime/Incident Report (*Continued*)

STATE PRISON USA
CRIME/INCIDENT REPORT
PART B—INVOLVED PARTIES

FORM 840-B

Institution/Facility	Date Occurred	Time Occurred	Incident Log Number
State Prison USA 4B2R/SHU, Exercise Yard #2	**10/22/03**	**0855**	**STA-04B-98-5910**

Inmates

Name (Last, First, MI)				Sex	Ethnicity	Class Score
N/A						

Check one ☐ Victim ☐ Suspect ☐ Witness	Inmate Number	CII #	FBI #	SS #	PV. RTC?
	Date Received by Prison	Date Received by State	Anticipated Release Date	Date of Birth	Housing Assignment

Commitment Offenses (Optional)	County of Commitment
Description of Injuries	Prison Gang/Disruptive Group (Validated)

Check All That Apply
☐ Hospitalized   ☐ Treated and Released   ☐ Refused Treatment   ☐ Deceased   Location of Hospital/Treatment

Name (Last, First, MI)				Sex	Ethnicity	Class Score
N/A						

Check One ☐ Victim ☐ Suspect ☐ Witness	Inmate Number	CII #	FBI #	SS #	PV. RTC?
	Date Received by Prison	Date Received by State	Anticipated Release Date	Date of Birth	Housing Assignment

Commitment Offenses (Optional)	County of Commitment
Description of Injuries	Prison Gang/Disruptive Group (Validated)

Check All That Apply
☐ Hospitalized   ☐ Treated and Released   ☐ Refused Treatment   ☐ Deceased   Location of Hospital/Treatment

Staff, Visitors, Others

Name (Last, First, MI)	Title	Sex	Ethnicity	Regular Days Off
Holmes, S.	**Correctional Off.**	**M**	**White**	**S/S**

Check One ☐ Victim ☐ Suspect ☐ Witness	Check One ☐ Staff ☐ Visitor ☐ Other ___	Badge/I.D. # **46817**	Post Assignment **I.S.U**	I.D. # **P95931**
		Description of Injuries **N/A**		

Check All That Apply **N/A**
☐ Hospitalized   ☐ Treated and Released   ☐ Refused Treatment   ☐ Deceased   Location of Hospital/Treatement **N/A**

Name (Last, First, MI)	Title	Sex	Ethnicity	Regular Days Off
Hurtado, X.	**Correctional Off.**	**M**	**Hispanic**	**T/F**

Check One ☐ Victim ☐ Suspect ☐ Witness	Check One ☐ Staff ☐ Visitor ☐ Other ___	Badge/I.D. # **73049**	Post Assignment **4B2L #1**	I.D. # **W609100**
		Description of Injuries **N/A**		

Check All That Apply **N/A**
☐ Hospitalized   ☐ Treated and Released   ☐ Refused Treatment   ☐ Deceased   Location of Hospital/Treatment **N/A**

Name (Last, First, MI)	Title	Sex	Ethnicity	Regular Days Off
Pyle, F.	**Correctional Off.**	**M**	**Black**	**F/S**

Check One ☐ Victim ☐ Suspect ☐ Witness	Check One ☐ Staff ☐ Visitor ☐ Other ___	Badge/I.D. # **02449**	Post Assignment **4B2R #1**	I.D. # **W0498**
		Description of Injuries **N/A**		

Check All That Apply **N/A**
☐ Hospitalized   ☐ Treated and Released   ☐ Refused Treatment   ☐ Deceased   Location of Hospital/Treatment **N/A**

Crime/Incident Report (*Continued*)

STATE PRISON USA
SUPPLEMENTAL TO THE CRIME/INCIDENT REPORT (FORM 839)

Page 1 of 2 Pages

Name (Last, First, MI) **Thomas, P.**	Badge/I.D. # **35135**	Date Occurred **10/22/03**	Incident Log Number **STA-04B-98-5910**

Length of Service **11 yrs 8 mos**	I.D. # **P122285**	Post Description **4B2R Yard Gunner**	Time Occurred **0855**	Report Date **10/22/03**

Days Off **F/S**	Duty Hours **0600/1400**	Incident Location **4B2R/SHU, Exercise Yard #2**

Description of Incident/Crime **Battery on Inmate with S.B.I.**	Code of Regulations Section/Rule **3005 c**

Your Role	Witnesses (Preface: S-Staff, V-Visitor, O-Other)		Inmates Involved (Preface: S-Suspect, V-Victim, W-Witness)	
☐ Primary	**C/O Pyle**	**MTA Helpful**	**Brown**	
☐ Responder	**C/O Womack**	**MTA Kit**	**Black**	
☐ Witness	**C/O Groeneveld**	**C/O Munoz**	**White**	
☐ Victim	**Sgt. Vogelsman**	**C/O Hurtado**		
☐ Camera	**Sgt. Zedillo**			

Force Used by You	Less Lethal Weapons	Lethal Weapons	Number of Rounds Fired	Force Observed by You
☐ Lethal	☐ 37mm **D-13445**	☐ Mini-14	_____	☐ Lethal
☐ Less lethal	Serial #	☐ Shotgun	_____	☐ Less lethal
☐ Physical	☐ Baton	☐ Handgun	_____	☐ Physical
☐ None	☐ OC	☐ Other	_____	☐ None
	☐ Other			

Evidence Collected	Evidence Description	Disposition	Weapon	Bio Hazard
☐ Yes ☐ No	**2, 37mm Blocks**	**Evidence Locker, 4B2R**	☐ Yes ☐ No	☐ Yes ☐ No

Reporting Staff Injured	Description of Injury	Location Treated	Bodily Fluid Exposure
☐ Yes ☐ No			☐ Yes ☐ No

Narrative:

On 10-22-03 at approximately 0855 hours, while performing my duties as the 4B2R Exercise Yard Gunner, I observed two inmates, White and Black, commit the crime of battery on Inmate Brown. Inmate White, K-52489, 4B2R-07R, and Inmate Black, J-89660, 4B2R-18L, had a brief discussion and then approached Inmate Brown, K-25791, 4B2R-04L. White and Black simultaneously began striking Brown in the head and upper torso with their clinched fists, knocking Brown to the ground. I immediately began giving verbal orders to stop fighting and get down with negative results. I then discharged one 264W multiple baton round from my state issue 37mm launcher, serial number D-13445, ricocheting the wooden blocks approximately nine feet in front of the combatants, with negative results. White and Black continued their assault on Brown as he lay in a fetal position with both arms over his head trying to protect himself. I again discharged one 264W round, ricocheting the wooden block approximately nine feet in front of the combatants, with negative results. Brown was now lying on his right side in a limp manner, apparently unable to protect himself as Black began kicking him in the head. Seeing Brown's apparent unconsciousness, I drew my state-issue Ruger Mini-14 rifle, serial number 18660030, from its assigned gun rack. I gave the warning, "Stop fighting; I have the Mini." Both White and Black then stopped the attack.

Reporting Staff Signature **Thomas, P.**	Date **10/22/03**

Reviewer's Signature **Incharge, I.**	☐ Approved ☐ Clarification Needed	Date **10/22/03**

Supplemental to Crime/Incident Report

62

Name (Last, First, MI)	Badge/I.D. #	Date Occurred	Incident Log Number
Thomas, P.	**35135**	**10/22/03**	**STA-04B-98-5910**

☐ Continuation of Report   ☐ Additional information   ☐ Clarification request

Narrative:

   Both combatants were recalled from the yard, placed in separate holding cells and medically cleared by MTA K. Jones. Inmates White and Black were re-housed without further incident. Due to Brown's injuries and inability to safely exit the yard on his own, he was assisted by Sergeants Zedillo and Vogelsman and Officers S. Womack, E. Munoz, and C. Groeneveld. Brown was removed from the yard on a stokes litter and brought into the rotunda where MTA J. Scott medically examined him. Brown was then referred to the Acute Care Hospital for further medical treatment. All wooden blocks and evidence were recovered and secured per institutional procedures.

Reporting Staff Signature			Date
Thomas, P.			**10/22/03**

Reviewer's Signature	☐ Approved	☐ Clarification Needed	Date
Incharge, I.			**10/22/03**

Supplemental to Crime/Incident Report (*Continued*)

STATE PRISON USA
SUPPLEMENTAL TO THE CRIME/INCIDENT REPORT (FORM 839)

Page __1__ of __1__ Pages

Name (Last, First, MI) **Zedillo, E.**	Badge/I.D. # **26213**	Date Occurred **10/22/03**	Incident Log Number **STA-04B-98-5910**

Length of Service **15 yrs 7 mos**	I.D. # **P95823**	Post Description **4B2R Facility Sergeant #1**	Time Occurred **0855**	Report Date **10/22/03**

Days Off **S/M**	Duty Hours **0600-1400**	Incident Location **4B2R/SHU, Exercise Yard #2**

Description of Incident/Crime **Battery on Inmate with S.B.I.**	Code of Regulations Section/Rule **3005 c**

Your Role	Witnesses (Preface: S-Staff, V-Visitor, O-Other)		Inmates Involved (Preface: S-Suspect, V-Victim, W-Witness)	
☐ Primary	**C/O Thomas**	**MTA Helpful**	**Brown**	
☐ Responder	**C/O Womack**	**MTA Kit**	**Black**	
☐ Witness	**C/O Munoz**	**Sgt. Vogelsman**	**White**	
☐ Victim	**C/O Groeneveld**	**Lt. Incharge**		
☐ Camera	**C/O Hurtado**			

Force Used by You	Less Lethal Weapons	Lethal Weapons	Number of Rounds Fired	Force Observed by You
☐ Lethal	☐ 37mm _____	☐ Mini-14 _____		☐ Lethal
☐ Less lethal	Serial #	☐ Shotgun _____		☐ Less lethal
☐ Physical	☐ Baton	☐ Handgun _____		☐ Physical
☐ None	☐ OC	☐ Other _____		☐ None
	☐ Other			

Evidence Collected	Evidence Description	Disposition	Weapon	Bio Hazard
☐ Yes ☐ No			☐ Yes ☐ No	☐ Yes ☐ No

Reporting Staff Injured	Description of Injury	Location Treated	Bodily Fluid Exposure
☐ Yes ☐ No			☐ Yes ☐ No

Narrative:

On Thursday 10/22/03 at approximately 0855 hours while assigned as the 4B Sergeant #1, I responded to a personal alarm in 4B2R. When I arrived I was informed that a fight had occurred on the 4B2R Exercise Yard #2. After observing that Inmate Brown, K-25791, 4B2R-04L, was not following my orders and staggering while on his feet and falling down again. I instructed two uninvolved inmates off the yard first. I then instructed the aggressors, Inmates White, K-52489, 4B2R-18L, and black, J-89660,4B2R-07R, to leave the yard one at a time. I followed and handcuffed them and placed them in separate holding cells. Brown was still incoherent, so I instructed officers S. Womack, E. Munoz, and C. Groeneveld and Sergeant Vogelsman to assist Brown. These officers placed Brown on a stokes litter and took him to the Acute Care Hospital so that a Medical Technical Assistant could medically examine him. MTA Scott examined Brown and determined that he had sustained head injuries that were not life-threatening but were serious enough that Brown was kept in the Acute Care Hospital for observation. MTA Scott also examined White and Black in their holding cells. White has no injuries. Black had minor injuries to his left ankle and right shoulder. White's left tennis shoe and Black's right tennis shoe were taken as evidence as both had blood stains.

Reporting Staff Signature **Zedillo, E.**			Date **10/22/03**
Reviewer's Signature **Incharge, I.**	☐ Approved	☐ Clarification Needed	Date **10/22/03**

Supplemental to Crime/Incident Report (sample 2)

STATE PRISON USA
SUPPLEMENTAL TO THE CRIME/INCIDENT REPORT (FORM 839)

Page __1__ of __1__ Pages

Name (Last, First, MI) **Vogelsman, A.**	Badge/I.D. # **35883**	Date Occurred **10/22/03**	Incident Log Number **STA-04B-98-5910**

Length of Service **10 yrs 2 mos**	I.D. # **P15745**	Post Description **4B Facility Sergeant #2**	Time Occurred **0855**	Report Date **10/22/03**

Days Off **F/S**	Duty Hours **0600-1400**	Incident Location **4B2R/SHU, Exercise Yard #2**

Description of Incident/Crime **Battery on Inmate with S.B.I.**	Code of Regulations Section/Rule **3005 c**

Your Role	Witnesses (Preface: S-Staff, V-Visitor, O-Other)		Inmates Involved (Preface: S-Suspect, V-Victim, W-Witness)	
☐ Primary	**Lt. Incharge**		**Brown**	
☐ Responder	**Sgt. Zedillo**		**Black**	
☐ Witness	**C/O Thomas**		**White**	
☐ Victim	**C/O Womack**			
☐ Camera	**C/O Groeneveld**			

Force Used by You	Less Lethal Weapons	Lethal Weapons Number of Rounds Fired	Force Observed by You
☐ Lethal	☐ 37mm _____	☐ Mini-14 _____	☐ Lethal
☐ Less lethal	Serial #	☐ Shotgun _____	☐ Less lethal
☐ Physical	☐ Baton	☐ Handgun _____	☐ Physical
☐ None	☐ OC	☐ Other _____	☐ None
	☐ Other		

Evidence Collected	Evidence Description	Disposition	Weapon	Bio Hazard
☐ Yes ☐ No			☐ Yes ☐ No	☐ Yes ☐ No

Reporting Staff Injured	Description of Injury	Location Treated	Bodily Fluid Exposure
☐ Yes ☐ No			☐ Yes ☐ No

Narrative:

On 10/22/03 at approximately 0855 hours, I responded to an alarm from unit 4B2R. On arrival I supervised the removal of Inmates White, K-52489, 4B2R-18L, and Black, J-89660,4B2R-07R, from Exercise Yard #2. At this time Sergeant Zedillo, 4B Sergeant #1, informed me that the sole remaining inmate on yard #2, Brown, K-25791, 4B2R-04L, appeared to be seriously injured and needed immediate assistant. Sergeant Zedillo, Officers Munoz, Womack, and Groeneveld and I formed an impromptu medical extraction team and, accompanied by Lieutenant I. Incharge, entered Yard #2. Brown was clearly disoriented when we approached him, but he was non-resistive and cooperative. Team members placed him on a stokes litter and removed him from yard #2. Brown was then driven, with escort, to the Acute Care Hospital for treatment for head injuries.

Reporting Staff Signature **Vogelsman, A.**			Date **10/22/03**
Reviewer's Signature **Incharge, I.**	☐ Approved	☐ Clarification Needed	Date **10/22/03**

Supplemental to Crime/Incident Report (sample 3)

Page 1 of 1 Pages

Name (Last, First, MI) **Womack, B.**		Badge/I.D. # **36148**	Date Occurred **10/22/03**	Incident Log Number **STA-04B-98-5910**
Length of Service **4 yrs 11 mos**	I.D. # **P93866**	Post Description **4B2L Floor Office #2**	Time Occurred **0855**	Report Date **10/22/03**
Days Off **F/S**	Duty Hours **0600-1400**	Incident Location **4B2R/SHU, Exercise Yard #2**		

Description of Incident/Crime **Battery on Inmate with S.B.I.**	Code of Regulations Section/Rule **3005 c**

Your Role	Witnesses (Preface: S-Staff, V-Visitor, O-Other)		Inmates Involved (Preface: S-Suspect, V-Victim, W-Witness)	
☐ Primary	**Sgt. Zedillo**		**Brown**	
☐ Responder	**Sgt. Vogelsman**		**Black**	
☐ Witness	**C/O Groeneveld**		**White**	
☐ Victim	**C/O Munoz**			
☐ Camera	**MTA Helpful**			

Force Used by You	Less Lethal Weapons	Lethal Weapons Number of Rounds Fired		Force Observed by You
☐ Lethal	☐ 37mm _____	☐ Mini-14 _____		☐ Lethal
☐ Less lethal	Serial #	☐ Shotgun _____		☐ Less lethal
☐ Physical	☐ Baton	☐ Handgun _____		☐ Physical
☐ None	☐ OC	☐ Other _____		☐ None
	☐ Other			

Evidence Collected	Evidence Description	Disposition	Weapon	Bio Hazard
☐ Yes ☐ No	**1 Left State Issued Tennis Shoe. Size 9. Blood Stain on Toe**	**Submitted into Evidence Locker #5, Level 4.**	☐ Yes ☐ No	☐ Yes ☐ No

Reporting Staff Injured	Description of Injury	Location Treated	Bodily Fluid Exposure
☐ Yes ☐ No			☐ Yes ☐ No

Narrative:

On Thursday, 10/22/03, at approximately 0855 hours while performing my duties as Floor Officer #2, 4B2L, I responded to a alarm coming from 4B2R. The alarm was activated in response to a yard fight on Exercise Yard #2. After all of the aggressors and uninvolved inmates were removed from the yard, Sergeant E. Zedillo ordered me to go into the Security Housing Unit #2 with other staff and the stokes litter to retrieve the victim, Inmate Brown, K-25791, 4B2R-04L, because he was disoriented and could not leave the yard under his own power. Inmate Brown was lying immobilized and flat on his back so we (the hasty team) lifted Brown on the count of three onto the stokes litter. We carried Brown off the yard and placed him on the floor of the unit rotunda, where he was to be examined by MTA J. Scott. At this time I was ordered by Sergeant Vogelsman to go examine Inmate Black's (J-89660) tennis shoes. Inmate Black was in the building hallway holding cell alone. inmate Black gave me his tennis shoes, and I noticed blood stains on the left shoe toe. I took possession of the shoe and placed the #9 shoe in an evidence bag and submitted the evidence into Level 4 Evidence Locker #5 as per institutional procedure.

Reporting Staff Signature **Womack, B.**	Date **10/22/03**	
Reviewer's Signature **Incharge, I.**	☐ Approved ☐ Clarification Needed	Date **10/22/03**

Supplemental to Crime/Incident Report (sample 4)

STATE PRISON USA
SUPPLEMENTAL TO THE CRIME/INCIDENT REPORT (FORM 839)

Name (Last, First, MI) **Munoz, T.**	Badge/I.D. # **35023**	Date Occurred **10/22/03**	Incident Log Number **STA-04B-98-5910**

Length of Service **10 yrs. 6 mos**	I.D. # **P15811**	Post Description **4B2L Floor Officer #3**	Time Occurred **0855**	Report Date **10/22/03**

Days Off **S/M**	Duty Hours **0600-1400**	Incident Location **4B2R/SHU, Exercise Yard #2**

Description of Incident/Crime **Battery on Inmate with S.B.I.**	Code of Regulations Section/Rule **3005 c**

Your Role	Witnesses (Preface: S-Staff, V-Visitor, O-Other)		Inmates Involved (Preface: S-Suspect, V-Victim, W-Witness)	
☐ Primary	**Sgt. Zedillo**		**Brown**	
☐ Responder	**Sgt. Vogelsman**		**Black**	
☐ Witness	**C/O Womack**		**White**	
☐ Victim	**C/O Groeneveld**			
☐ Camera	**MTA Helpful**			

Force Used by You	Less Lethal Weapons	Lethal Weapons Number of Rounds Fired		Force Observed by You
☐ Lethal	☐ 37mm _____	☐ Mini-14 _____		☐ Lethal
☐ Less lethal	Serial #	☐ Shotgun _____		☐ Less lethal
☐ Physical	☐ Baton	☐ Handgun _____		☐ Physical
☐ None	☐ OC	☐ Other _____		☐ None
	☐ Other			

Evidence Collected	Evidence Description	Disposition	Weapon	Bio Hazard
☐ Yes	**1 Right Tennis Shoe**	**Submitted into Evidence**	☐ Yes	☐ Yes
☐ No	**with Blood Stains**	**Locker #5, Level 4**	☐ No	☐ No

Reporting Staff Injured Description of Injury	Location Treated	Bodily Fluid Exposure
☐ Yes		☐ Yes
☐ No		☐ No

Narrative:

On 10/22/03 at approximately 0855 hours, while performing my duties as the 4B2L Floor Officer #3, I responded to a personal alarm at 4B2R. The alarm had been activated due to a yard fight on Exercise Yard #2. After the aggressors and the uninvolved inmates were removed from the yard, Sergeant Zedillo, the Facility Sergeant, ordered me to go with the other assembled staff to Yard #2 with the stokes litter to retrieve the victim, Inmate Brown, K-25791, 4B2L-04L. Brown was in a sitting position toward the back wall of the yard. As we entered the yard, Sergeant Zedillo ordered Brown to lie down on his back. Brown complied and we lifted him onto the litter. I assisted with carrying Brown in the litter off the yard, where he was placed in the unit rotunda where MTA J. Scott examined him. Brown was sent to the Acute Care Hospital for further examination. Sergeant Zedillo then ordered me to report to the rotunda holding cell where I found Brown alone. I had Brown removed his right tennis shoe which had blood stains near the toe of the shoe and the shoe lace. I placed the shoe in an evidence bag and submitted it into Evidence Locker #5 at the Level 4 Evidence Room per institutional procedures.

Reporting Staff Signature **Munoz, T.**			Date **10/22/03**
Reviewer's Signature **Incharge, I.**	☐ Approved	☐ Clarification Needed	Date **10/22/03**

Supplemental to Crime/Incident Report (sample 5)

STATE PRISON USA
SUPPLEMENTAL TO THE CRIME/INCIDENT REPORT (FORM 839)

Page __1__ of __1__ **Pages**

Name (Last, First, MI) **Groeneveld, C.**	Badge/I.D. # **58007**	Date Occurred **10/22/03**	Incident Log Number **STA-04B-98-5910**

Length of Service **2 yrs. 8 mos**	I.D. # **56743**	Post Description **4B2R Floor #3**	Time Occurred **0855**	Report Date **10/22/03**

Days Off **T/W**	Duty Hours **0600-1400**	Incident Location **4B2R/SHU, Exercise Yard #2**

Description of Incident/Crime **Battery on Inmate with S.B.I.**	Code of Regulations Section/Rule **3005 c**

Your Role	Witnesses (Preface: S-Staff, V-Visitor, O-Other)		Inmates Involved (Preface: S-Suspect, V-Victim, W-Witness)	
☐ Primary	**Sgt. Zedillo**		**Brown**	
☐ Responder	**Sgt. Vogelsman**		**Black**	
☐ Witness	**C/O Munoz**		**White**	
☐ Victim	**C/O Womack**			
☐ Camera	**C/O Pyle**			

Force Used by You	Less Lethal Weapons	Lethal Weapons Number of Rounds Fired	Force Observed by You
☐ Lethal	☐ 37mm _____	☐ Mini-14 _____	☐ Lethal
☐ Less lethal	Serial #	☐ Shotgun _____	☐ Less lethal
☐ Physical	☐ Baton	☐ Handgun _____	☐ Physical
☐ None	☐ OC	☐ Other _____	☐ None
	☐ Other		

Evidence Collected	Evidence Description	Disposition	Weapon	Bio Hazard
☐ Yes			☐ Yes	☐ Yes
☐ No			☐ No	☐ No

Reporting Staff Injured	Description of Injury	Location Treated	Bodily Fluid Exposure
☐ Yes			☐ Yes
☐ No			☐ No

Narrative:

On Thursday, 10/22/03, at approximately 0855 hours, while performing my duties as the 4B2R Floor Office #3, I was assisting with B-1 yard release when the unit alarm was activated. I responded to the yard sallyport door. After Sergeant A. Vogelsman, Sergeant E. Zedillo, Officer R. Womack, Officer E. Munoz, and I had removed all of the uninvolved inmates from the yard, we entered the yard with a stokes litter to retrieve Inmate Brown. Sergeant E. Zedillo instructed me to help lift Brown onto the stokes litter. I then assisted in lifting and moving Brown through the sallyport to the rotunda area. MTA J. Scott medically examined Brown, and S.Holmes of the Investigative Services Unit photographed Brown and the crime scene area. Approximately 5 minutes later, I assisted in moving Brown, still secured to the stokes litter, to a state vehicle parked just outside of the unit door. After placing Brown in the vehicle, I accompained Brown to the Acute Care Hospital for examination, where I remained for observation and security.

Reporting Staff Signature **Groeneveld, C.**			Date **10/22/03**
Reviewer's Signature **Incharge, I.**	☐ Approved	☐ Clarification Needed	Date **10/22/03**

Supplemental to Crime/Incident Report (sample 6)

SUPPLEMENTAL TO THE CRIME/INCIDENT REPORT (FORM 839)

Page __1__ of __1__ Pages

Name (Last, First, MI) **Hurtado, X.**	Badge/I.D. # **73049**	Date Occurred **10/22/03**	Incident Log Number **STA-04B-98-5910**
Length of Service **4 yrs. 3 mos.**	I.D. # **W609100**	Post Description **4B2L Floor #1**	Time Occurred **0855**	Report Date **10/22/03**

Length of Service **4 yrs. 3 mos.**	I.D. # **W609100**	Post Description **4B2L Floor #1**	Time Occurred **0855**	Report Date **10/22/03**

Days Off **T/F**	Duty Hours **0600-1400**	Incident Location **4B2R/SHU, Exercise Yard #2**

Description of Incident/Crime **Battery on Inmate with S.B.I.**	Code of Regulations Section/Rule **3005 c**

Your Role	Witnesses (Preface : S-Staff, V-Visitor, O-Other)		Inmates Involved (Preface: S-Suspect, V-Victim, W-Witness)	
☐ Primary	**Sgt. Zedillo**	**MTA Kit**	**Brown**	
☐ Responder	**Sgt. Vogelsman**		**Black**	
☐ Witness	**C/O Groenveld**		**White**	
☐ Victim	**MTA Helpful**			
☐ Camera				

Force Used by You	Less Lethal Weapons	Lethal Weapons Number of Rounds Fired	Force Observed by You
☐ Lethal ☐ Less lethal ☐ Physical ☐ None	☐ 37mm _____ 　　　Serial # ☐ Baton ☐ OC ☐ Other	☐ Mini-14 _____ ☐ Shotgun _____ ☐ Handgun _____ ☐ Other _____	☐ Lethal ☐ Less lethal ☐ Physical ☐ None

Evidence Collected	Evidence Description	Disposition	Weapon	Bio Hazard
☐ Yes ☐ No			☐ Yes ☐ No	☐ Yes ☐ No

Reporting Staff Injured	Description of Injury	Location Treated	Bodily Fluid Exposure
☐ Yes ☐ No			☐ Yes ☐ No

Narrative:

On Thursday, 10/22/03, at approximately 0855 hours, while performing my duties as 4B2L Floor Officer #2, I responded to a personal alarm in 4B2R. On arrival Sergeant E. Zedillo instructed me to assist with escorting Inmate Brown, K-25791, 4B2R-04L, to the Acute Care Hospital. Inmate Brown had been involved in a physical altercation on the yard. I observed that Brown had received numerous injuries to his head. I assisted the other officers with placing Brown in the stokes litter. Correctional Officer M. Groeneveld and I moved Inmate Brown from the rotunda area to a state vehicle parked outside the unit door and accompanied him to the Acute Care Hospital for examination. Subsequently Brown was treated and released back to custody and re-housed without further incident.

Reporting Staff Signature **Hurtado, X.**			Date **10/22/03**
Reviewer's Signature **Incharge, I.**	☐ Approved	☐ Clarification Needed	Date **10/22/03**

Supplemental to Crime/Incident Report (sample 7)

STATE PRISON USA
SUPPLEMENTAL TO THE CRIME/INCIDENT REPORT (FORM 839)

Name (Last, First, MI) **Pyle, A.**		Badge/I.D. # **49204**	Date Occurred **10/22/03**	Incident Log Number **STA-04B-98-5910**
Length of Service **4 yrs. 7 mos.**	I.D. # **P99408**	Post Description **4B2R Floor #1**	Time Occurred **0855**	Report Date **10/22/03**
Days Off **F/S**	Duty Hours **0600-1400**	Incident Location **4B2R/SHU, Exercise Yard #2**		

Description of Incident/Crime **Battery on Inmate with S.B.I.**	Code of Regulations Section/Rule **3005 c**

Your Role	Witnesses (Preface: S-Staff, V-Visitor, O-Other)		Inmates Involved (Preface: S-Suspect, V-Victim, W-Witness)	
☐ Primary	**Sgt. Zedillo**		**Brown**	
☐ Responder	**Sgt. Vogelsman**		**Black**	
☐ Witness	**C/O Thomas**		**White**	
☐ Victim	**C/O Womack**			
☐ Camera	**MTA Helpful**			

Force Used by You	Less Lethal Weapons	Lethal Weapons	Number of Rounds Fired	Force Observed by You
☐ Lethal	☐ 37mm _____	☐ Mini-14 _____		☐ Lethal
☐ Less lethal	Serial #	☐ Shotgun _____		☐ Less lethal
☐ Physical	☐ Baton	☐ Handgun _____		☐ Physical
☐ None	☐ OC	☐ Other _____		☐ None
	☐ Other			

Evidence Collected	Evidence Description	Disposition	Weapon	Bio Hazard
☐ Yes ☐ No			☐ Yes ☐ No	☐ Yes ☐ No

Reporting Staff Injured	Description of Injury	Location Treated	Bodily Fluid Exposure	
☐ Yes ☐ No			☐ Yes ☐ No	

Narrative:

On Thursday, 10/22/03, at approximately 0855 hours, while assigned to 4B2R Floor #1, I went upstairs to the 4B2R control booth to push buttons for yard release. After releasing approximately five inmates, I noticed Correctional Officer P. Thomas activate his personal alarm, and he ordered the yard to get down. I then secured the sallyport door. Ensuring that no inmates were in the sallyport, I went over to the 4B2R Exercise Yard #2 window to observe the disturbance. I observed two unknown black inmates, later identified as White, K-52489, 4B2R-18L, and Black, J-89660, 4B2R-07R, kicking and striking with clenched fists another unidentified black inmate, later identified as Brown, K-25791, 4B2R-04L, in the head and upper torso. Correctional Officer P. Thomas gave several verbal orders to "get down" with negative results. Correctional Officer P. Thomas then discharged one round from his state issued 37mm launcher with negative results. Inmate Brown, who was in a fetal position attempting protect himself, appeared to be knocked unconscious. C/O Thomas continued to order the yard to "get down" with negative results. C/O Thomas fired a second 37mm round with negative results. Fearing for the safety of Inmate Brown, C/O Thomas drew his state issued Mini-14 and continued to order the inmates to get down. At this point they complied. All of the inmates, with the exception of Brown, were removed from the yard. Brown seemed to regain consciousness, but he was dazed and incoherent. Several staff personnel then proceeded onto the yard with the stokes litter and removed Brown from the yard.

Reporting Staff Signature **Pyle, A.**			Date **10/22/03**
Reviewer's Signature **Incharge, I.**	☐ Approved	☐ Clarification Needed	Date **10/22/03**

Supplemental to Crime/Incident Report (sample 8)

CORRECTIONAL REPORT WRITING EXERCISES

Now it is time for you to actually write two sample correctional reports. These two reports are not as detailed as the sample report you just reviewed. You will be given all of the facts, circumstances, and persons involved in the incidents. It will be your task to choose the proper forms from Appendix B and write the report. *Make sure your reports are complete, accurate, concise, and grammatically correct. These are all areas that your instructor will use to grade your report.*

Correctional Report Writing Exercise 1

The crime committed is Battery on an Inmate with a Weapon. The Section/Code is 3005 ©. The incident occurred at State Prison #2, Building 2R, Facility IV-A, Exercise Yard #1, on 4/6/03 at 0944 hours. There was no SERT Activated, no Negotiation Team Activated, no Mutual Aid Request, and no Media Notified. There were no Deaths. The incident was an Assault on one inmate by two others. The type of Assault was a beating and slashing. There was no serious injury to anyone. The inmate weapon was a slashing instrument. There were no shots fired. There were no Controlled Substances, no Lockdowns, and no Exceptional Activity. Incident Log #SP-4A-99-0161.

The following were the persons involved:

Inmates

Victim
Bernardo, James I. Male, Indian, Class Score-52, Inmate #K-27654, CII #A5421, FBI #2765KAZ, SSN 281-61-7768, PV RTC-No, Date Received by prison-2/24/99, Date Received by State-3/20/98, Anticipated Release Date-9/23/2004, DOB-10/4/68, Housing Assignment-4A2R-18L, Commitment Offense-Transportation/Sales of a Controlled Drug, County of Commitment-Ventura, Description of Injuries-"Refer to Medical Reports," Prison Gang . . . N/A

Suspect
Ortega, Jesus, Male, Hispanic, Class Score-245, Inmate #H-15866, CII #A7865431, FBI #N/A, SSN- 566-19-3841, PV RTC-No, Date Received by Prison-3/5/99, Date Received by State-10/8/91, Anticipated Release Date-4/4/2022, Date of Birth-1/12/73, Housing Assignment-4A2R-14R, Commitment Offense-Attempted Murder 2nd with Weapon, County of Commitment-Los Alamos, Description of Injuries-Abrasions to both knees; Reddened areas to the upper chest, Prison Gang . . . N/A

Suspect
Moreno, Juan, Male, Hispanic, Class Score-77, Inmate #K-51127, CII #A887346, FBI

#56589VA8, SSN-561-73-7138, PV RTC-No,
Date Received by Prison-2/8/99, Date Received
by State-5/28/97, Anticipated Release Date-
11/18/2004, DOB-12/31/71, Housing
Assignment-4A2R-15R, Commitment Offense-
Robbery 2nd, County of Commitment-Orange,
Description of Injuries-Abrasions to both knees,
cut/laceration to left bicep and elbow, Prison
Gang . . . N/A

Staff/Visitors/Others

Witness	Gonzalez, Jack, Correctional Officer, Male, Hispanic, Regular Days Off-F/S, Badge #39817, Post Assignment-4A2R Gunner, ID #P26458
Witness	Strong, I.R., Correctional Sergeant, Male, White, F/S, 39817, 4A Sergeant, P51186
Witness	Helpful, I.M., MTA, Female, White, S/M, 46258, 4AMTA #1&2, P26689
Witness	Williams, Wayne, Correctional Officer, Male, White, S/S, 21391, 4A2R Floor, P18659
Witness	Hamilton, Greg, Correctional Officer, Male, White, S/T, 40631, 4A2R Floor, P98196
Witness	Bustamonte, Andrew, Correctional Officer, Male, Hispanic, S/S, 37676, 4A2R Floor, P46961
Witness	Holmes, S.I., Correctional Officer, Male, White, S/S, 46751, I.S.U., P29816
Witness	Watson, D.R., Correctional Officer, Male, White, S/S, 43604, I.S.U., P12084
Witness	Scope, I.C., Medical Doctor, Male, White, S/S, Badge #-N/A, Post Assignment-Acute Care Hospital, ID #E-72586
Witness	Mendoza, Paul, Correctional Officer, Male, Hispanic, S/S, 36781, 4A2R Floor, P52281

SUMMARY OF INCIDENT

Occurred April 6, 2003 at approximately 0941 hours. Battery on
Inmate with Weapon. Facility IV-A, Bldg 4A2R, Exercise Yard #1,
during White/Southern Mexican Controlled/Compatible Yard
period. Report based on written reports (Forms 839) of staff
involved. Officer J. Gonzalez monitoring inmates. Observes
Inmates Moreno and Ortega viciously attack Inmate Bernardo by
striking him with their fists in his face, head, back, and upper
torso. Gonzalez yells, "stop and get down." Negative results.
Moreno and Ortega continue assault on Bernardo, who has hands

up in front of his face. Attempting to block blows from attack. Officer Gonzalez reached for 37 mm Launcher, less than lethal weapon. Inserts one 264W cartridge. Officer Williams activated the unit alarm for response. Gonzalez again yelled to inmates to "get down" and raised the weapon and pointed it out between the bar window. Inmates saw weapon; immediately got down in a prone position on ground. Correctional Sergeant I.R. Strong responded to unit. Was apprised of the incident. Instructed Gonzalez to "recall the yard," beginning with the victim first, aggressors, and finally noninvolved inmates. Responding staff (Hamilton, Bustamonte, Mendoza) assisted with escorting inmates back to their housing units. Bernardo taken to the Acute Care Hospital. Moreno and Ortega placed in separate holding cells, pending medical examinations and clearance for re-housing. MTA I.M. Helpful medically examined and cleared Inmates Moreno and Ortega back to their housing. Medical Doctor I.C. Scope completed an evaluation on Inmate Bernardo at the ACH and cleared him for re-housing within Facility IV-A. Bernardo sustained a one inch slash on top of the head, an open laceration to this right eye, a swollen lip, slashes to the right side of the back and left side of the chest. Moreno received small abrasions to both knees, lacerations to left biceps and right elbow, and a cut to right hand middle finger. Ortega received abrasions to both knees and reddened areas to upper right chest area. After clearance, all inmates returned to assigned cells. Slashing and puncture wound on the victim are consistent with a weapon being involved (refer to medical report on Inmate Bernardo attached). I.S.U. Officers S. Holmes and D. Watson responded. Conducted thorough search of the yard for weapon(s) or contraband-negative results. All inmates involved declined to give an explanation for the fight. Review of Bernardo's Central File reflects that neither of the aggressors were on his enemy list (Form 830). Review of the Forms 120 revealed that all of the inmates involved were approved for the exercise yard program by the Institution Classification Committee (I.C.C.). Rules Violations Reports (Form 125) were issued charging Moreno and Ortega with violation of the Code of Regulations, Section 3005 ©. Officers prepared a victim's chronology of events for Bernardo. Moreno and Ortega were placed on his enemy list (Form 830) and removed from the "B-1" Controlled/Compatible yard pending program review by ICC. These Rules Violation Reports will be processed in accordance with Departmental policies and Procedures. This matter will be referred to the county district attorney's office for felony prosecution if deemed appropriate after review by the Investigative Lieutenant. I informed all of the appropriate administrative staff and the institutional investigator of this incident. News media not informed. I shall keep you (State) informed of any further developments in this matter via Supplemental Report (s).

You are I.M. Incharge, Correctional Lieutenant, Reporting Officer, 32816, 13 years 0 months, 4/8/03. The authorizing signature is I.B. Mean, Facility Captain. You are to prepare the Forms 840-A, B, and C plus the Medical Report of Injury and the Medical Diagram Form on Bernardo. There may be grammatical, style, syntax, and other errors in the sample narrative above. You must prepare your report in correct English grammar.

Correctional Report Writing Exercise 2

The crime is Trafficking a Controlled Substance (Marijuana). The location is State Prison #2, Facility III-B, Building 05, Cell #205. The date and time of occurrence is 03/03/03 at 1030 hours. The Code Section is 3016, Stimulants, Sedatives, Controlled Substances. The following were *not* utilized: SERT, Negotiation Team, Mutual Aid, Media. Under "Related Information," none of these is applicable.

Inmates Involved

Suspect	Pothead, Marvin A., Male, Black, Class Score-74, Inmate # D-93685, CII# A0897748, FBI# N/A, SSN-558-42-2222, PV RTC-No, Date Received by Prison-09/24/89, Date Received by State-08/23/88, Anticipated Release Date-Lifer, Date of Birth-09/08/70, Housing Assignment-3B05-205L, Commitment Offenses-Murder, 2nd, County o Commitment-Los Feliz, Description of Injuries-None Noted, Prison Gang . . . -None Noted, Treated and Released, III-B MTA Clinic
Suspect	High, Ira M., Male, Black, Class Score-160, Inmate #-C-97968, CII#-A00681281, FBI#69567AA3, SSN-555-55-5555, PV RTC-yes, Date Received by Prison-09/10/98, Date Received by State-11/07/83, Anticipated Release Date-02/09/2022, Date of Birth-11/07/64, Housing Assignment-3B05-205U, Commitment Offenses-Assault with a Deadly Weapon, County of Commitment-Los Feliz, Description of Injuries-None Noted, Prison Gang . . . None Noted, Treated and Released, III-B MTA Clinic

Staff/Visitors/Others

Witness	Faraday, Jim E., Correctional Lieutenant, Male, White, T/F, 6803, III-B Lieutenant, P27866, N/A, N/A, N/A
Witness	Ball, Irving T., Correctional Officer, Male, Black, S/M, 46686, 3B05 Floor Officer, P99512, N/A, N/A, N/A

Witness	Incharge, Ivan B., Correctional Sergeant, Male, Black, S/M, 34121, III-B Sergeant, P22117, N/A, N/A, N/A
Witness	Hurry, Norman A., Correctional Officer, Male, Hispanic, S/S/H, 35989, I.S.U., P16575, N/A, N/A, N/A
Witness	Teammate, Igor B., Correctional Officer, Male, White, S/S/H, 34639, I.S.U., P60990, N/A, N/A, N/A
Witness	Landry, Greg T., Correctional Officer, Male, Black, S/S, 36025, III-B Floor #1, P62991, N/A, N/A, N/A
Witness	Helpful, Mary R., MTA, Female, Black, F/S, 40397, III-B Medical Clinic, N/A, N/A, N/A
Witness	Pulse, Arthur G., MTA, Male, White, S/M, 67688, III-B Medical Clinic, N/A, N/A, N/A

SUMMARY OF INCIDENT

Irving T. Ball's Narrative. Conducting routine cell search in housing unit 3B05, cell #205. Occupied by Inmates Pothead and High. Discovered one (1) bindle of a green leafy substance wrapped in clear cellophane. Stored in the finger slot of a medical latex glove. Location-bed frame of the upper bunk approximately 4 inches to the left of the pillow and 1 inch from the end of the bunk. Second green leafy matter in bindle on top of the desk in cell 3B05-205. Third bindle hidden under the upper left corner of the state issued pillow at the head of the upper bunk. I left and secured cell 205, and I notified the Facility 3B Sergeant, I.B. Incharge, 34121, of my findings. Correctional Officer G. Landry, 36025, placed both Pothead and High in handcuffs and immediately escorted them to the Facility 3B Program Officer's holding cells. Sergeant Incharge notified I.S.U. Correctional Officers Hurry and Teammate, and they responded to the scene. Hurry conducted field test. Positive for marijuana. Teammate took control of the evidence. To be sent to Mid-Valley Toxicology Laboratory for further identification.

Greg T. Landry's Narrative. Wednesday, March 3, 2003 approximately 1030 hours. Collecting inmate appeals forms. III-B housing unit's appeal boxes. I entered housing unit 3B05 to discover Correctional Officer I. Ball conducting a cell search on the second tier, cell #205. Officer I. Ball instructed me to come to the doorway of cell #205. C/O I. Ball informed me that he had discovered a substance resembling marijuana. I. Ball directed me to Inmates Pothead, D-93685, and High, C-97968, who occupy cell #205. Who were seated at the dayroom tables in "A" Section. I ordered both inmates to stand, and I conducted a clothed body search of each inmate. I found no further evidence or contraband on them. Placed Inmates

Pothead and High in handcuffs. Escorted them to the facility III-B Program Office. Where they were placed in holding cells

Jim E. Faraday's (Facility Lieutenant) Narrative. On Wednesday, March 3, 2003 at approximately 1030 hours, Correctional Officer I. Ball discovered three separate quantities of marijuana. Totaling 02.158 grams Housing unit 3B05, cell #205. Assigned to Inmates Pothead, D-93685, 3B05-205L and High, C-97968, 3B05-205U. While performing a routine search of cell 3B05-205. Correctional Officer I. Ball discovered one (1) latex glove. Containing two (2) cellophane wrapped bindles of a green leafy substance. This bindle was located on the metal frame. Of the upper bunk. Approximately four (4) inches to the left of the state issue pillow and approximately one (1) inch from the end of the upper bunk. Second bindle on top of the desk within the cell. Third bindle under the upper left corner of the state issue pillow at the head of the upper bunk. No other contraband was discovered during the search. C/O I. Ball secured the cell and apprised Correctional Sergeant I.B. Incharge, 34121, III-B Sergeant of the discovery. Contacted Correctional Officers N. Hurry and I Teammate, Investigative Services Unit. Responded to Housing Unit 3B05. Sergeant Incharge and Officer Ball escorted Officers Hurry and Teammate to cell 205. Cell door released. Officer Hurry took three (3) polaroid photographs showing two (2) bindles on the desk area and one (1) bindle on the upper bunk area. Officer Hurry conducted presumptive field test. Utilizing Narcotic Identification Kit (N.I.K.). Test proved positive for marijuana. Officer Teammate took control of the contraband. Itemized the items as follows; One (1) clear cellophane bindle containing a green leafy substance and one (1) latex glove (MA01); one (1) white paper bindle containing a green leafy substance (MA02); one (1) white paper bindle containing a green leafy substance (MA03). Officer Teammate maintained sole possession of the contraband items until he processed them as evidence into the level III Sub-Evidence Room, Locker #50. In accordance with Institutional Procedures. Correctional Officer G. Landry, 36025, placed Inmates Pothead and High in handcuffs. Escorted them to the Facility III-B Program Office. Where they were placed in holding cells. Inmates Pothead and High were medically cleared. By Senior Medical Technical Assistant M. Helpful, 40397, and Medical Technical Assistant (MTA) A. Pulse, 67688, respectfully. Neither inmate had any visible injuries. Inmates Pothead and High were medically cleared. Subsequently placed in the Administrative Segregation Unit without further incident. There were no staff or inmate injuries incurred as a result of this incident On Tuesday, March 9, 2003 the suspected marijuana was sent to Mid-Valley Toxicology for laboratory analysis. On Tuesday, March 16, 2003, State Prison #2's Investigative Services Unit received written confirmation that the substance submitted for testing was, in fact, marijuana. With a combined weight of 02.158 grams (three bindles; MA01 = 01.976 grams; MA02 = 0.68 grams; MA03 = 0.114 grams). Rules Violation Reports (Form 116) were issued Log Number 3B-99-03-041 and 3B-99-03-042. Charging

Inmates Pothead and High with violation of the Code of Regulations, Section 3016 (a), Stimulants, Sedatives and Controlled Medications, for the specific act of Trafficking Controlled Substance. These Rules Violation Reports will be processed in accordance with Institution Policy and Procedures. This incident will be referred to the County District Attorney's Office for possible felony prosecution if deemed appropriate after review by the Investigative Lieutenant. All appropriate administrative staff and the institutional investigator were informed of this incident, the news media was not. All procedural requirements have been met. You will be apprised of any further developments via supplemental reports.

You must now prepare your report. Prepare *all* appropriate forms to make this report complete. A caution is in order: There are grammatical, style, and syntax errors in the sample narratives above. You must prepare the narrative of your report in correct English. You are Correctional Lieutenant Jim E. Faraday, 6803, 16 years, 6 months, 3/18/03. The Facility Captain is I.B. Mean.

COMMON CORRECTIONAL TERMS, SLANG, AND ACRONYMS

13: Southern California gang association ("SUR 13")

14: Northern California gang association ("Norte," "XIV")

37 mm: 37-mm gas launcher gun

AB: Aryan Brotherhood prison gang

ACHI: Heroin

AD-SEG: Administrative segregation

AKA: Also known as; moniker; street or gang name

ANT: Anti-narcotic testing

AOD: Administrative officer of the day

AOR: Parole agent of record

ASSOCIATE: Affiliated with a prison gang

AW: Associate warden

B&W: Bread and water

BACKING: Support or protection from gang or other inmates

BANDERA: Gang colors; symbol; flag

BANGER: Street or prison gang member

BARRIO: Neighborhood in the community

BEEF: Problem; rule violation; crime

BGD: Black Gangster Disciples

BGF: Black Guerrilla Family

BLA: Black Liberation Army (terrorist group)

BLADE: Inmate's sharpened manufactured instrument

BLOOD IN/OUT: Gang expectation to kill to join, and to be killed on attempt to leave

BLOODS: Street gang (originated in the Los Angeles area); non Crips; red gang color

BO: Marijuana

BONDS: Rules of conduct for the Northern Structure prison gang

BOOK: Flee; run; arrest; assault

BORDER BROTHER: Hispanic inmate from Mexico

BPT: Board of Prison terms

BRO: Brother; friend; fellow gang member

BUD: Marijuana

BULLDOG: Street gang (originated in Fresno); red gang color

BULLET: One year in custody

BUM RAP: Innocent of the charge or rumors

BURN: Deceive; cheat; fail to keep promise

BUS RIDE: Transferred to another location or institution

BUSTED: Apprehended; caught in the act; arrested

BUSTER: Rival gang member; not a real gangster

BUZZED: Intoxicated or under the influence of narcotics

C&PR: Classification and Parole Representative

CADILAC: Coffee with cream and sugar; single bunk

CALIFAS: California

CANTEEN: Prison store

CAP: Shoot someone

CAPT.: Captain

CAPPO: Leader in an organized crime family

CARNAL: Member of a Hispanic prison gang; fellow member

CAT J: Inmate with psychiatric problems

CCWPT: Concurrent with present term

CDW: Chief deputy warden

C-File: Inmate central file; main prison records

CHALE: No

CHEESE: Informant; rat

CHINA WHITE: Heroin from Asia

CHIPPING: Using minimum amount of narcotics

CHIVA: Heroin

CHOLO: Young male gang member

CHOTA: Law enforcement

CHRONO: Report of classification action

CHUCO: Older gang member; "Pachuco"; zoot suiters of the 1940s

CI: Confidential informant

CLASSIFICATION: Panel that reviews inmates' housing program needs

CLEAN: No contraband or weapons

CLIQUE: Gang

CMO: Chief medical officer

CO: Correctional officer

COLD: Dead; unexpected; old information

COLORS: Colored clothing identifying specific gang membership

CON: Convict; convicted inmate

CONTRACT: Orders or payment to assault or murder someone

COUNT: Counting inmates at correctional facilities

CRACK: Cocaine processed into a rock-like substance

CRANK: Methamphetamines/ amphetamines ("Speed")

CRETE: Firearm

CRI: Confidential reliable informant

CRIB: Residence; home; cell

CRIP: Street gang (originated in Los Angeles area); blue gang color

CSR: Classification service representative

CSWPT: Consecutive with present term

CTF: Correctional training facility, Soledad

CTQ: Confined to quarters

CUMSUM: Cumulative case summary

CUZ: Fellow Crip gang member

DAM: Departmental administrative manual

DANCING: Fighting

DATE: Scheduled parole or release date

DEAD MAN: Inmate housed on death row; threat to kill

DEAD PRESIDENTS: U.S. currency

DEAR JOHN: Letter relative to the termination of a relationship or marriage

DE-BRIEF: Procedural interview to drop out of a prison gang

DIME: Ten dollars; inform/tell staff members

DISS: Disrespect someone

DMS: Daily movement sheet

DO: Ex-gang member/dropout

DOC: Department of Corrections

DOM: Departmental operations manual

DPA: Department of Personnel Administration

DRB: Discharge Review Board

DRD: Discharge review date

DRESSED: Wearing gang attire

DRIVE-BY: Shooting from a moving vehicle

DSL: Determinate sentencing law

DUCKATS: Inmate money; pass

DUST: Kill; PCP

DVI: Duel vocational institution, Tracy

EEO: Equal employment opportunity

EME: "M"; Mexican Mafia

ENE: "N"; Nuestra Familia

EPTT: Employee Post Trauma Team

ESSEY: General reference by Hispanic male inmates

EXTRACTION: Forcible removal from a cell

FARMERS: Members of the Nuestra Familia prison gang; Northern Hispanic

FISH: New inmate; new staff member

FISH KIT: Items issued to new arrivals

FISH LINE: String used to pass and retrieve items

FIVE-O: Law enforcement

FLAG: Display gang symbol, bandanna, or handkerchief

"G": Gangster

GASSING: Throwing liquids or body fluids on staff members

GET DOWN: Fight; assume a prone position on the ground

GOON SQUAD: Security squad members

GP: General population

GREEN LIGHT: Authorization to assault or kill someone

H&S: Health and safety code

HA: Hells Angels motorcycle gang

HACK: Correctional officer

HAT: Bad standing with gang; targeted for assault

HEAT: Law enforcement

HIT: Planned or ordered assault

HIT LIST: List of persons to be assaulted or killed

HOLE: Administrative segregation

HOME BOY: Friend or associate

HOOD: Neighborhood

HORSE: Heroin

HOUSE: Prison housing/cell

IA: Internal Affairs

ILLING: Sick

INS: Immigration and Naturalization Service

ISL: Indeterminate sentencing law

ISP: Ironwood State Prison, Blythe

IST: In-service training

ISU: Investigative Service Unit/Security Squad

IWF: Inmate welfare fund

JACK: Confront; rob; assault

JACKET: Commitment offense(s); reputation

JOINT: Marijuana cigarette; correctional facility

JUMPED IN: Joined a gang

KEISTER: Hide items inside body cavities

KEY: Kilo of cocaine

KITE: Letter or note

L&L: Lewd sex acts with children

LA RAZA: Mexican or Hispanic race

LEG BAIL: Flee on foot

LIFER: Inmate sentenced to life in prison

LOCKDOWN: Inmates confined to cells and cancellation of activities

LOCKUP: Request for protective housing

LOP: Loss of privileges due to disciplinary action

LT.: Lieutenant

MAC: Men's advisory committee

MAD DOG: Stare or attempt to intimidate by body language

MAIL DROP: Location in the community where mail is rerouted

MAIN LINE: General population housing

MAN: Law enforcement

MAYATE: Hispanic gang slang for a black person

MCSP: Mule Creek State Prison, Ione

MEPD: Minimum eligible parole date

MERD: Minimum eligible release date

MESA: Table; leaders of the Nuestra Familia/Nuestra Raza/Northern Structure

MINI: Ruger Mini-14 rifle

MOU: Memorandum of understanding

MTA: Medical technical assistant

"N" NUMBER: Civil commitment

NAEA: Narcotic Addict Evaluation Authority

NF: Nuestra Familia prison gang

NLR: Nazi Low Riders prison gang

NMT: Negotiation Management Team

NORTANO: Hispanic inmate from Northern California

NORTE: North

NS: Northern Structure prison gang

OC: Oleoresin capsicum/pepper spray; organized crime

OFF: Kill

OG: Original gangster/senior member

OP: Operation procedures

ORWD: Off-reservation work detail

OTC: Out to court

P&CSD: Parole and Community Service Division

PA: Program administrator; parole agent

PACKING: Carrying a weapon, narcotics, or other contraband

PAL: Parolee-at-large

PAR REV: Parole revoked

PAT DOWN: Clothed body search

PAY NUMBER: Inmate job with a salary

PC: Penal code; protective custody

PEED: Failed to fight or follow orders

PHU: Protective housing unit

PIA: Prison Industry Authority

PIECE: Weapon; shank; knife

PIG: Law enforcement

PIG PEN: Area designated for staff members only

PIG STICKER: Stabbing instrument intended for staff members

PILE: Weight pile area

PIN (PEN): Correctional facility

PO: Probation officer; police officer

POBOR: Peace Officer's Bill of Rights

POC: Parole outpatient clinic

POINT MAN: Lookout for approaching staff members

PROGRAM: Institutional rules, regulations, and procedures

PRUNO: Inmate-made wine

PV: Parole violator

PVRTC: Parole violator returned to custody

PVSP: Pleasant Valley State Prison, Coalinga

PVWNT: Parole violator with new term

QUEEN: Homosexual inmate

R&R: Revocation and Release Unit

RAG: Colored handkerchief indicative of gang membership

RAL: Release-at-large (civil commitment)

RAT: Informant

REP: Employee union representative; reputation

RIG: Hypodermic syringe and related paraphernalia

ROW: Death row at San Quentin State Prison

RRD: Revocation release date

RTC: Returned to custody

RUCA: Girlfriend; wife

RUSH: Charge; attack

SAFE HOUSE: Residence in the community used to sanction fugitives

SALLYPORT: Security gates that only open one at a time

SANCHO: General name for person having an affair with wife/girlfriend

SERT: Special Emergency Response Team

SET: Specific neighborhood in larger street gangs

SGT.: Sergeant

SHAKEDOWN: Search of large areas/housing units

SHANK: Inmate-manufactured stabbing/slashing device

SHIV: Inmate-manufactured stabbing instrument

SHOTCALLER: Leader or person in charge

SHU: Security Housing Unit

SIGN: Display gang hand symbols

SISSY: Homosexual male inmate

SLAMMED: Lockdown status; confined to housing units; injected narcotics

SLAMMER: Correctional facility

SLEEPER: Undercover (active) gang member

SLIPPIN: Making mistakes

SLOB CRIP: Name for Bloods street gang member

SMACK: Heroin

SMOKED: Assaulted, shot, or killed someone

SNITCH: Informant; rat; stoolie

"S" NUMBER: Temporarily housed at a state prison for safe keeping

SOFT YARD: General population housing for inmates with safety concerns

SORT: Federal prison's Special Operations Response Team

SPB: State Personnel Board

SQUARE: Cigarettes; nongang member

SRB: Shooting Review Board

SRT: Shooting Review Team

SSU: Special Service Unit

STICK: Stab

STINGER: Used to heat water

STREETS: Community

STRIP: Unclothed body search

SUR: South

SURENO: Hispanic inmate from Southern California

SWP: Supreme or superior white power

TAGGING: Graffiti

TCL: Temporary community leave

TIER TENDER: Inmate porter; cleaner on the tiers

TIP: Inmate's gang affiliation

TITLE 15: Director's rule book

TRUSTEE: Low-security-risk inmate worker

TS: Texas Syndicate prison gang

TURNED OUT: Sexually assaulted

TURNKEY: Correctional officer

UNLOCK: Inmates released from housing units

USINS: U.S. Immigration and Naturalization Service

UZI: Any semi-automatic firearm

VALIDATED: Documented prison gang member

VATO: General reference between Hispanic gang members

VC: Vehicle code

W&I: Welfare and institution code

WACKED: Assaulted; under the influence of PCP

WAKE UP: Day of an inmate's release

WALLS: Inside a correctional facility

WARDEN: Person in charge of a state prison

WIRE: Written message, note, or orders

"W" NUMBER: Female inmate

WOLF TICKETS: Bragging or threatening beyond capabilities

YACA: Youth and Adult Correctional Agency

YARD: Recreation; exercise yard

YARD RECALL: Inmates returned from the yard to assigned housing units

YOPB: Youthful Offender Parole Board

ZOOM ZOOM & WAM WAM: Sweets or snacks

6

Testifying in Court

What makes a police or correctional officer an effective witness in court? The single most important characteristic of effective testimony is *professionalism*. Specifically, a police or correctional officer's effectiveness in court depends in large measure on whether he demonstrates those qualities that judges and jurors expect in a professional police or correctional officer.

The good news is that these qualities can be developed. Although a particular officer's personality may make him more likable, the overall impact of the officer's testimony seems to hinge on habits and traits that can be cultivated. In this chapter we will explore several things that have proven to be successful in court.

PREPAREDNESS

The Boy Scouts are absolutely right; you must be prepared! The amount of preparation that is necessary will, of course, depend on the seriousness of the case and the nature and scope of the testimony you will be giving.

Read the Police or Correctional Officer Report

An officer cannot be an effective witness unless he has a command of the facts in the report. This does not mean he has to memorize the report. By no means should an officer memorize things such as license plate numbers and quotes from the victim or defendant; this will sound rehearsed and phony. Before you testify, you want to look at your report so the jurors know they are getting exactly what was said. You would be safe if you memorized some details such as dates, times, day of the week, or other routine facts.

Read Transcripts

If you have given testimony in the case previously (e.g., at a preliminary hearing or a 1538.5 hearing [California]), obtain a copy of the transcript from the district attorney and read it over carefully.

This will help refresh your memory about the facts, and you may notice something you said that was incorrect. If you do notice something, the jury should hear this from the district attorney, not from the defense attorney or public defender.

Talk to the District Attorney

In every case, a pretrial or prehearing meeting between the officer and the district attorney is absolutely essential. Normally this will take only a few minutes; however, in a complicated case, it may take hours. The purpose of this meeting is to review the facts of the case, discuss the subjects that will be covered on direct and cross-examination, and try to anticipate any problems that might arise.

Visit the Scene

It is certainly not necessary for an officer to visit the scene of the crime or the arrest in every case. However, it may be a good idea in some cases; for example, if you may be asked to draw a diagram in court or describe the physical layout or characteristics of the area, an on-site visit might be helpful.

IMPARTIALITY

An officer's testimony will have significantly greater weight with a judge or jury if the officer demonstrates an impartial, unbiased attitude. Conversely, an officer's credibility will suffer if it appears that he has a personal interest in the outcome of the case. The most effective officer witness will answer each question truthfully, even if the answer might hurt the prosecution's case. If an officer equivocates on something he thinks will hurt the case, it will probably emerge from the testimony of other witnesses. This will possibly negate the officer's credibility. A common tactic by defense attorneys is to ask a hypothetical question that could be answered either "A" or "B." "A" helps the prosecution; "B" helps the defense. Some officers will only answer "A" because "A" is more supportive of the district attorney's case. Generally "A" and "B" are both plausible. Answering emphatically "A" will only cause a loss of credibility.

Treat the District Attorney and Defense Attorney Alike

Officers can also demonstrate impartiality by dealing with the defense attorney in the same manner as the district attorney. The worst approach to testifying is to appear friendly and relaxed when being questioned by the district attorney but become clearly defensive when being cross-examined by the defense attorney. The following are some signs in body language that signal bias: a change in the tone of voice; some movement in the witness chair; a loss of eye contact; a reply of "Yes, sir" to the district attorney but a reply of "That is correct, Counselor" to the defense attorney. If the district attorney misstates something, the officer should correct him just as he would correct the defense attorney.

Do Not Be Evasive

An officer's credibility may also be hurt if he attempts to avoid answering an unambiguous question. Judges and jurors usually see this as an indication that the officer has an interest in the outcome of the case and that the answer may help the defense. Below is an example of an exchange between an officer and a defense attorney that makes this point:

> *Attorney*: Where were you standing when you allegedly saw my client drop the cocaine?
> *Officer*: What do you mean, "Where was I standing?"

When officers are evasive in their testimony, they look defensive. Good defensive attorneys will continue to ask the question until they get a direct answer. Eventually an officer will have to answer the question, but it makes a very bad impression on the judge and the jury.

Do Not Volunteer Information

Just as an attempt to avoid answering a question may hurt an officer's credibility, an attempt to volunteer information that was not solicited may indicate to the judge or jury that the officer is trying to assist the prosecution. In other words, an attempt to volunteer information tends to indicate that the officer is not an impartial witness.

An effective police or correctional officer witness just answers the questions that are asked. Officers do not get into long explanations; if officers do get into lengthy explanations, it gives the defense attorney more options. It makes the officers look as though they are not neutral. If officers show susceptibility to volunteering information, a good defense attorney will challenge them and try to impugn their credibility.

Request to Explain an Answer

Although an officer should not volunteer information that was not requested, it is quite proper to request to explain an answer if an explanation is necessary to prevent misunderstanding. For example, suppose a robbery victim told the officer, "The guy who robbed me was six feet tall." The six-foot-tall officer then asks, "So, he was about my height?" The victim responds, "No, he was two or three inches shorter than you." The robber is later arrested, and he is exactly five feet ten inches tall. At the robber's trial, the defense attorney asks, "Isn't it a fact the victim told you the robber was six feet tall?"

Technically, the answer to the question is *yes* because the victim did, in fact, say the robber was six feet tall. What should you do as an officer confronted with this situation?

1. Answer "Yes."
2. Answer "Yes"; then quickly try to explain the rest of the victim's statement before the attorney objects.
3. Answer "Yes"; then ask for permission to explain the answer.

The subject-matter experts will tell you that the best approach is answer C. B is clearly the worst answer because it appears you are trying to mitigate the effect of your "Yes" answer. Your response might be, "The answer is yes, but with the court's permission, I would like to explain this answer to prevent misunderstanding."

SELF-CONTROL

Here is one of the most important—and most difficult—things an officer can do to be an effective witness: refuse to demonstrate anger toward the defense attorney. There are two reasons why this is important. First, the officer's image as an unbiased, impartial witness will be damaged if the officer exhibits hostility toward the defense attorney. Second, the officer's anger will make it difficult for him to think clearly and to effectively respond to the attorney's questions.

On the other hand, if the officer successfully resists the impulse to demonstrate anger—no matter how exasperating the defense attorney—the officer's image as a professional will be strengthened. Poise and self-control are qualities that judges and jurors like to see in police and correctional officers.

Do Not Get Sarcastic or Irritable

Instead of demonstrating outright anger, officers sometimes respond to probing defense attorneys by getting sarcastic or irritable. This must also be avoided. Common expressions that officers use when engaged in this behavior are "Of course I did" or "As I have already told you." When an attorney is making you mad, do not give in. Your anger will keep you from thinking clearly. If he can upset you, he is winning.

DEFENSE ATTORNEY TRAPS

There are many ways a defense attorney may try to damage an officer's credibility or to simply cause confusion. In most cases, these tactics are entirely proper and ethical. After all, an important part of the defense attorney's job is to test the credibility of every person who testifies against his client. Oftentimes, however, the effectiveness of an officer's testimony is reduced for reasons that have nothing to do with truth and accuracy.

Confusing Questions

Attorneys frequently ask questions that are confusing. When this happens, do not hesitate to respond, "I do not understand that question." Under no circumstances should you guess at the meaning of a question. Do not be afraid to ask for clarification because the jury probably did not understand the question either.

Repeated Questions

Attorneys may try to cause officers to give inconsistent answers by asking the same question several times. Some attorneys will ask the same question three or four times. Essentially it is the same question, but there's a slight change in the language. They are trying to get a "Yes" answer to a question that was previously answered with a "No." When this happens and the district attorney does not object, you should respond with "I think you asked that question earlier."

Repeated Answers

Attorneys may ask a series of questions that, for one reason or another, the officer cannot answer. If this happens to you, try to avoid giving the same response to each question. An officer who immediately responds "I do not recall" or "I do not remember" to a series of questions may be viewed as being evasive or uncooperative. As an alternative, you should give each question some thought and try to respond as directly as possible. For example, rather than saying "I do not recall," you might say, "I did not notice," "I did not see that," or "I was not looking at that."

Summary of Previous Testimony

Be especially alert when a defense attorney asks a question in which he summarizes your previous testimony: "Earlier you testified that. . . ." The danger here is that the attorney may deliberately or negligently misstate your earlier testimony. If so, and if you answer the attorney's question, it may appear that you agree with the attorney's summary of your testimony. You can easily see the ramifications, so do not allow yourself to get caught in this trap. You should say, "That's not what I said" and then proceed to give your actual testimony.

Times and Distances

Attorneys frequently ask an officer to estimate the amount of time it took to do something. This can cause problems if the officer is just guessing instead of making a considered estimate. The problem you may be faced with here is that your guess may be in conflict with time estimates given by other witnesses. The best approach is to verbally walk yourself through the event, estimating the time of each movement. For example:

Bad

Attorney: How long did it take?
Officer: I don't know.
Attorney: Was it five minutes?
Officer: I guess so.

Good

Attorney: How long did it take?
Officer: I'm not sure, but I think I can figure it out.
Attorney: Okay.
Officer: Well, I got out of my patrol car and walked up to Mr. Suspect. That would have taken about 10 seconds. Then I asked to see his driver's license. He took out his driver's license, and I looked at it. That took about 20 to 30 seconds. That's when he pulled out the gun. So I would estimate it took 30 to 40 seconds.

Cross-Examination Concerning the Accuracy of Police Reports

Defense attorneys frequently attempt to create doubt about an officer's testimony by pointing to differences between the testimony and what the officer said in his police report. For example, there may be inconsistencies between the testimony and the police report, or the officer may testify about something that was not included in the report. If this happens to you, you must remember—do not become defensive. *If there is an error in your police or correctional report, admit it. If you forgot to include something in your report that should have been included, say so.*

It may be difficult to admit a mistake on the witness stand, but it is a lot better than trying to cover up or make excuses. There is a natural tendency to think that the judge or jurors will not believe anything else you say on the stand. On the contrary, judges, jurors, and attorneys know that you are human and fallible so this will prove your honesty.

Sometimes an officer will not include certain information in a police or correctional report because it did not seem important at the time. If that is why you did not put the information in your report, just be honest and say so. A police or correctional report is not meant to chronicle every detail of the event. When defense attorneys discover that you have testified to something that is not in your report, they may use the following tactic: "Officer, you have received training in writing reports. This is a copy of your report. Can you show me where I can find the information you just testified to?" Your response to this should be to explain that your report simply describes what happened and provides enough information to establish probable cause and to get the case charged. You are not expected to put every conceivable detail in the report. *Never respond to a question regarding something that was omitted by saying, "I did not have the time."* This will give the judge and jury the impression that the case is not important to you.

Answer of "I Do Not Know"

If you do not know the answer to a question, say so. Do not guess. There is nothing wrong with answering, "I don't know," or "I can't remember."

Plain English

There is virtually nothing that irritates a judge or jury as much as hearing officers speak in a stuffy, military-type style that has become associated with law enforcement. In Chapter 3, I referred to this as stilted. It is characterized by the use of words and phrases that are unnatural and overly formal in place of words and phrases that are simple and direct. Below are some examples of stilted (and clear) language:

- I exited my patrol vehicle. (I got out of my patrol car.)
- I proceeded northbound. (I drove north.)
- I activated my emergency equipment. (I turned on my red lights and siren.)
- I effectuated a right turn. (I turned right.)
- After the arrest of the suspect was consummated . . . (After I arrested Mr. . . .)
- I entered the residence. (I went into the house.)
- I had occasion to talk to the suspect. (I talked to Mr. . . .)
- That is correct. (Yes.)

OTHER SUGGESTIONS

Here are some other suggestions that seem to be universally helpful for officers giving testimony:

- Appear interested in the questions, as opposed to just saying "Yes" and "No" in a flat monotone. Make your testimony alive for the jury.
- Do not lounge in the witness chair. Sit straight or lean slightly forward.
- Be thoughtful when answering questions. For example, if the district attorney shows you a gun and asks, "Is this the gun?" do not just perfunctorily say "Yes." Look at the gun carefully. If there is something distinctive about the gun,

point it out: "I put my serial number on the gun. . . . Yes, here it is. This is definitely the gun."

- Talk to the jury. Look at the jurors and make eye contact with them when you are answering questions.
- Have a sense of humor on the witness stand. There is nothing wrong with letting the jury know you are human.
- Accept the fact that you may be nervous.
- Decide whether you want to put on your uniform to testify, even if you are off duty. This presents a more official image. Detectives who are normally in plainclothes wear their suits, and this is what jurors expect. Never wear jeans or casual clothes; the only exception would be officers who are working undercover.
- Refer to the defendant by name: Mr. _____. This sounds more professional and unbiased.
- Do not make statements that are merely conclusions (e.g., "I had probable cause to arrest," "He did not see me"). Instead, give the facts that caused you to reach this conclusion (e.g., "I believed I had probable cause to arrest because . . ." "I do not think he saw me because it was dark and he was looking in the other direction").
- State only your name when the court clerk asks you to state your name. Do not give your title, and do not spell your name until the clerk asks you to do so. It sounds ostentatious and makes you appear self-important.

If you follow all of the guidelines that have been discussed above, you should be a very effective witness in any case in which you testify.

Review of English Grammar, Syntax, and Construction

This section is designed for those users who wish to review the basics of good English prior to completing Section I.

Verb Forms and Tenses

INTRODUCTION

Verb forms and tenses begin our discussion of the basics of good English writing. As announced in the beginning of this text, these basics are presented in the programmed format or style. The answers to the frames are found at the end of each chapter.

VERB FORMS (FRAMES 1–13)

In English, verbs have three main forms or principal parts. In Frame 24, we shall discuss a fourth form, but our concentration will be on the three main forms:

1. English verbs have three _____ or _____.

FRAME 2

The three principal parts of a verb are present, past, and past participle. The present form of the verb is the common form of the verb.

FRAME 3

Now let's discuss the infinitive, which is often thought to be a verb or verb form. Infinitives will almost always begin with *to* followed by the simple form of the verb. Examples: to sneeze, to smash, to cry, to shriek. Because an infinitive is *not* a verb, you cannot add -*s*, -*es*, -*ed*, or -*ing* to the end. Infinitives can be used as nouns, adjectives, or adverbs.

Example: "*To sleep* is the only thing Officer Wilcox wants after working a graveyard shift on patrol." *To sleep* functions as a noun because it is the subject of the sentence. Identify how the infinitive is used in the following sentence:

1. When Officer Gilley responds to the scene of a shooting, he is unable to look at the blood so he turns his head and refuses *to look*. _____

FRAME 4

All verbs have three forms: present, past, and past participle. We will use the verb *work* as an example. The forms, or principal parts, of the verb are the following:

Present .... work (or works)
Past .... worked
Past participle .... worked

Since the verb *work* (or *works*) is a regular verb, you can make both the past and past participle forms by adding *-d* (if verb ends in *e*) or *-ed*. This is true for all regular verbs.

Write the forms of the regular verb *talk* below:

1. Present _____

2. Past _____

3. Past participle _____

FRAME 5

Regular verbs are verbs that add *-d* or *-ed* to make the past and past participle forms. This can serve as a test as to whether a verb is regular or irregular. If you can add *-d* or *-ed* to make the past and past participle forms, then the verb is regular.

Underline the regular verbs in the following group of words.

1. move   5. turn

2. think   6. erase

3. grow   7. know

4. believe

FRAME 6

Irregular verbs change in several different ways to make the past and past participle forms. For a small number of verbs, such as *burst* and *hit,* all three principal parts are the same. Sometimes the past and past participle forms are the same, but some verbs change their internal spelling to make past and past participle forms. Because the principal parts form in varying ways, we use the word *irregular* to describe such verbs. A verb is irregular when its past and past participle forms *do not* end with *-ed.*

1. We classify verbs according to the way they change to make the past and past participle forms. The two categories are _____ and _____ verbs.

FRAME 7

Here is a pattern, or system, to follow that will determine the three principal parts of a verb. Select a verb such as the verb *fly*. Example: Today they fly. Yesterday they flew. They have flown. This system works on both regular and irregular verbs.

Insert the correct form of *see* in each of the three blanks.

1. Present: Today they _____.

2. Past: Yesterday they _____.

3. Past participle: They have _____ for a long time. (Note: The word *have* is a helping verb.)

When we fit the verb *know* into the pattern, we find that the principal parts are *know, knew, known.*

What are the principal parts of the verb *see?*

1. Present _____

2. Past _____

3. Past participle _____

FRAME 8

Let's practice on a few common irregular verbs. The table below shows the present form; use the pattern to determine the past and past participle forms. Complete the table.

Present	Past	Past Participle
1. speak	_____	_____
2. eat	_____	_____
3. go	_____	_____
4. lose	_____	_____
5. drink	_____	_____
6. give	_____	_____
7. are	_____	_____

8. do _____ _____

9. dive _____ _____

FRAME 9

Note: The past and past participle forms of *lose* are the same; *dive* is either a regular or an irregular verb.

FRAME 10

Let's review what we have learned. There are three different forms, or principal parts, of a verb. The names of the principal parts are present (or infinitive), past, and past participle. We classify verbs according to the formation of principal parts. If the past and past participle are formed by adding -*ed*, the verb is a regular verb; all other verbs are irregular verbs.

Classify these verbs as regular or irregular; the left column shows the present form.

Present Form of Verb Classification

1. break _____

2. think _____

3. believe _____

4. worry _____

5. swim _____

6. weigh _____

FRAME 11

In the next few frames, we shall review some problem verbs. One such verb is *pay*. The principal parts are *pay*, *paid*, and *paid*. It sounds as if it is a regular verb, but it is not because the spelling is *paid* rather than *payed*.

FRAME 12

Set and *sit* are a pair of problem verbs. *Set* means to put or to place. The principal parts are *set, set,* and *set.* Examples:

They set the table.
Yesterday she set the table.
They have set the table many times.

Sit refers to resting or being seated. The principal parts are *sit*, *sat*, and *sat*. Examples:

They sit in their places.
Yesterday they sat at their places.
They have sat in their places.

1. If you intend the meaning to be to put or to place, then use the verb _____.

2. If you intend the meaning to refer to resting or being seated, then use the verb _____.

FRAME 13

Lay and *lie* are another pair of problem verbs. *Lay* means to set, put, or place. The principal parts are *lay*, *laid*, and *laid*. Examples:

They lay the books in place.
They laid the books in place.
They have laid the books in place.

Lie means to rest or to recline. The principal parts are *lie*, *lay*, and *lain*. Examples:

They lie on the beach.
Yesterday they lay on the beach.
They have lain on the beach all afternoon.

1. If you intend the meaning to be to set, to put, or to place, then use the verb _____.

2. If you intend the meaning to be to rest or to recline, then use the verb _____.

VERB TENSES (FRAMES 14–30)

Now we shall turn our attention to verb tenses. The reason for learning about the principal parts of verbs is that you should know about the principal parts before learning about tenses. When you have mastered both topics, you will be able to avoid errors related to verb forms or tenses.

There are six tenses. Of the six tenses, three are simple tenses and three are perfect tenses.

1. There are six tenses; three of the tenses are _____ and three are _____.

FRAME 15

Here are the names of the six tenses:

Simple	Present
Tenses	Past
	Future
Perfect	Present perfect
Tenses	Past perfect
	Future perfect

FRAME 16

The present tense uses the present form of the verb. We shall use the verb *work* as an example. The present form is *work*. Sometimes the present form has an -*s* at the end. Note these examples:

They work in the mine.
He works in the mine.

1. The present tense uses the _____ form of the verb.

FRAME 17

We use the present tense for these reasons:

To show action that is presently happening
To describe a situation that is presently true
To make a statement of generalization

Examples of each follow:

I write for the newspaper.
Henry is sick.
Fresh fruit tastes good.

In the item that follows, how is the present tense used?

1. Kelly does good work. _____

FRAME 18

The past tense uses the past form of the verb. Past tense refers to action completed in the past. We shall use the regular verb *talk* as an example; the past form is *talked*.

Identify the tense of each of the sentences below.

1. Henry believed everything his boss told him. _____

2. Joyce knows how to fix the machine. _____

3. Betty was ready when I arrived. _____

FRAME 19

The other simple tense is the future tense. It refers to action that will occur in the future. To form the future tense, use the present form of the verb and a helping verb, either *will* or *shall*. Example:

The police chief will promote six police officers to sergeant today.

Identify the tense of each sentence below.

1. Harry worked narcotics enforcement for eight years. _____

2. Detective Mann will return from the field interview at 1600. _____

3. The SWAT team will practice forced entries today at 1900. _____

FRAME 20

Let's review. There are three simple tenses: present, past, and future. The past tense uses the past form of the verb. Both present and future tenses use the present form of the verb.

Next, we shall consider the three perfect tenses: present perfect, past perfect, and future perfect. All the perfect tenses use the past participle form of the verb, and all the perfect tenses require one or more helping verbs.

1. The perfect tenses use the _____ form of the verb.

FRAME 21

The present perfect tense refers to action recently completed. We use the helping verb *has* or *have* to make the present perfect tense. Examples:

I have written to my mother.
John has finished the last course.

Identify the tense of each of the following sentences.

1. They sing in the choir. _____

2. Edward will see the picture next week. _____

3. Hal has seen all of the equipment. _____

FRAME 22

The past perfect tense, like all the perfect tenses, uses the past participle form of the verb. Use the helping verb *had* to form the past perfect tense. The past perfect tense shows action completed in the past before some other action or event occurred. Examples:

I had broken all the eggs before the cook arrived.
We had pushed the wall into place before it became a hazard.

Identify the tense of each of the following sentences.

1. He has painted the steps and deck. _____

2. She   painted   the   trim   around   the   windows.
_____

3. Bob   had   painted   the   overhang   before   he   left.
_____

FRAME 23

The future perfect tense uses two helping verbs, *will* and *have* (or *shall* and *have*), along with the past participle form of the verb. It refers to action completed at some future time. Example:

By Tuesday I shall have finished all the exercises.

Identify the tense of each of the following sentences.

1. She   had   worked   in   the   bakery   before   being   fired.
_____

2. They worry all the time. _____

3. Ken   will   have   completed   the   task   by   next   week.
_____

FRAME 24

At this point, we have learned that verbs have three principal parts used in the six tenses. Sometimes the present form ends in -s or -es. This is important when studying about agreement of subject and verb. At this time, note that you can add -ing to the present form of the verb. The -ing form is the present participle. (This is the fourth part mentioned in frame 1.) Although -ing is used in other ways, you can also use it to construct sentences in the present tense. Present participles complete progressive verbs or act as modifiers. Examples:

He is talking. (progressive verb)
I am thinking about it. (progressive verb)
You are his training officer. (modifier)

1. The present participle form of a verb ends in
_____.

FRAME 25

Closely associated with the present participle is another grammatical construction called the *gerund*. Gerunds *always* end in -ing. However, because they end in -ing, they are not so easy to pick out. Gerunds function as nouns. They will serve as subjects, subject complements, direct objects, indirect objects, and objects of prepositions. Examples:

Since Paul became a correctional officer, *training* new correctional officers has been his passion. (subject)
Paul's passion is *training*. (subject complement)
Paul enjoys *training* more than being with his family. (direct object)

FRAME 26

If you apply what you have learned, you will be able to avoid errors in tense. Let's look at some examples. Example of an error: He drawed a picture of the thief. This is an error because *draw* is an irregular verb with principal parts of *draw, drew,* and *drawn*. The sentence is in the past tense; it should use the past form, which is *drew*. The example corrected: He drew a picture of the thief.

Here is another example of an error. Write the corrected sentence below.

1. She knowed all the answers.

_____

FRAME 27

Here is another example of an error: Ben had drove the car into the ditch. This is an error because *drove* is the past form of the verb and the past form does not require a helping verb. Use helping verbs with the past participle forms. The error is corrected by removing the helping verb: Ben drove the car into the ditch.

Correct the following sentence.

1. I have saw many unusual things.

_____

FRAME 28

Another kind of error is a shift in tense. Example: Because he likes pizza, Joe ate at John's Pizza House. In the first part of the sentence, the verb *likes* is in the present tense; the other verb, *ate,* is in the past tense. Avoid such shifts in tense. Here is a correct version: Because he liked pizza, Joe ate at John's Pizza House.

Correct this sentence.

1. John walked into the house and speaks to his wife.

_____

FRAME 29

Frame 30 will be a short test of some of the things you have learned. First, let's review several important points:

1. Regular verbs are verbs that make their past and past participle forms by adding -*ed.*
2. Irregular verbs make their past and past participle forms in an irregular way according to no particular rule.
3. Past participle forms always require the use of one or more helping verbs.

FRAME 30

Test

Complete the table (questions 1–4).

Present	Past	Past Participle
1. demand	_____	_____
2. _____	threw	_____

3. fly   _____   _____

4. _____   _____   done

Circle the correct verb.

5. Sharon (broke, has broke) the vase.

6. Paul (speak, spoke) to the crew.

Identify the following as regular or irregular verbs.

7. begin _____

8. resign _____

9. move _____

10. see _____

QUIZ

1. In English, verbs have three main forms or principal parts. These three forms are _____, _____, and _____ _____.

2. Regular verbs are verbs that add _____ to make the _____ and _____ _____ forms.

3. Verbs are irregular when their _____ and _____ _____ forms _____ end with _____.

4. Past participle means that the action of the sentence happened
   a. yesterday.
   b. two days ago.
   c. over a period of time in the past.
   d. none of the above.

5. There are three simple tenses. They are _____, _____, and _____.

6. All of the perfect tenses use the _____ _____ form of the verb.

7. All of the perfect tenses require one or more _____ verbs.

8. True   False   Shifts in tense should be avoided.

9. To form the present perfect tense, you use the helping verb
_____ or _____ and the
_____ _____.

10. To form the future perfect tense, you use the two helping verbs
_____ and _____ (*or*
_____ and _____) and the
_____ _____.

11. The -*ing* form is the _____ _____.

ANSWERS TO FRAMES

Frame 1
1. forms   principal parts

Frame 3
1. direct object

Frame 4
1. Present—talk
2. Past—talked
3. Past participle—talked

Frame 5
1. move
4. believe
5. turn
6. erase

Frame 6
1. regular   irregular

Frame 7
1. Present—see
2. Past—saw
3. Past participle—seen

Frame 8

	Present	Past	Past Participle
1.	speak	spoke	spoken
2.	eat	ate	eaten
3.	go	went	gone
4.	lose	lost	lost
5.	drink	drank	drunk
6.	give	gave	given
7.	are	were	been
8.	do	did	done
9.	dive	dived (or dove)	dived

Frame 10
Classification
1. irregular
2. irregular
3. regular
4. irregular
5. irregular
6. regular

Frame 12
1. set
2. sit

Frame 13
1. lay
2. lie

Frame 14
1. simple
2. perfect

Frame 16
1. present

Frame 17

1. statement of generalization

Frame 18

1. past
2. present
3. past

Frame 19

1. past
2. future
3. future

Frame 20

1. past participle

Frame 21

1. present
2. future
3. present perfect

Frame 22

1. present perfect
2. past
3. past perfect

Frame 23

1. past perfect
2. present
3. future perfect

Frame 24

1. -ing

Frame 26

1. She knew all the answers.

Frame 27

1. I have seen many unusual things.
   or: I saw many unusual things.

Frame 28

1. John walked into the house and spoke to his wife or: John walks into the house and speaks to his wife.

Frame 30

	Present	Past	Past Participle
1.	demand	demanded	demanded
2.	throw	threw	thrown
3.	fly	flew	flown
4.	do	did	done
5.	broke		
6.	spoke		
7.	irregular		
8.	regular		
9.	regular		
10.	irregular		

8

Agreement of Subject and Verb

Chapter 8 is devoted to agreement of subject and verb. In order to do this, it will be necessary for you to learn about subjects, verbs, prepositional phrases, singular and plural subjects and verbs, tense, and some other related topics.

Just as in Chapter 7, most of the frames in this chapter require a response, and the correct answer is located at the end of the chapter. If you miss a question, go back and review the previous frame before continuing. It is imperative that you fully understand the current frame before moving on because each frame builds on the next. Ask your instructor to give you assistance if necessary.

Every sentence contains a subject and verb. The subject names someone or something. The verbs tell us what happened or tell us something about the subject. The subject and verb are basic building blocks of the English sentence. In order to be a complete sentence, *every* English sentence must contain both a subject and a verb. Also, all that is needed to make a complete sentence is a subject and a verb, although most sentences contain additional phrases, prepositions, adjectives, adverbs, etc.

1. Every English sentence contains a(n)
   _____ and _____.

In this frame, we will explain about subjects in more detail. The subject of a sentence often performs some action. Whoever or whatever performs the action will probably be the subject of the sentence. Here are some examples:

Henry washed the car.
Thomas Wolfe wrote several books.
The dog ate the food.

Select the subjects in sentences 1, 2, and 3 above.

1. _____

2. _____

3. _____

FRAME 4

In some sentences, the remainder of the sentence tells us more about the subject of the sentence. These sentences often use a form of the verb *to be* such as the following: is, are, was, were, has been. Here are some examples:

George is angry.
Margaret was ready at 7:00 P.M.
Red Prince looks as though he can run.

Select the subjects in sentences 1, 2, and 3 above.

1. _____

2. _____

3. _____

FRAME 5

In Chapter 2, Writing in the Active Voice, you learned about the active and passive voices. You learned that sentences should always be written in the *active voice* because subjects should *not* receive the action; they should be doing or performing the action of the sentence.

Rewrite the following sentences in the active voice.

1. Officer Williams was soaked by a summer shower.

   _____

   _____

2. Jack was burned by the grass fire.

   _____

   _____

FRAME 6

Here is a summary.

- A subject can perform an action.
- The rest of the sentence can describe the subject.
- A subject can receive action.

Classify each of the following sentences according to the function of the verb: performs an action, is described, or receives action.

1. Joe was tired and angry. _____

2. Emory hurried to his spot. _____

3. The rifle was assembled by an expert. _____

4. The frog leaped out of Bob's hand. _____

FRAME 7

Although there are exceptions to the rule, the subject is usually in the first part of the sentence. For example: The *editor* of the *newspaper* works at his *office*. Of the three italized words (all nouns), the word in the first part of the sentence is the subject.

1. The subject of a sentence is often in the _____ of a sentence.

FRAME 8

To make the subject agree with the verb, you must first identify the subject. Sometimes this is difficult because there is a prepositional phrase in the first part of the sentence. A prepositional phrase does not contain either a subject or a verb. It does, however, contain a preposition, an adjective (sometimes), and either a noun or a pronoun. Here are some examples of prepositional phrases:

- in the morning
- by myself
- at the end
- with George
- on the ceiling
- of the best
- as an actor
- through the field

FRAME 9

In the sentences that follow, underline the prepositional phrases.

1. As an actor, he was a failure.

2. In his spare time, Allen worked.

3. The leader of the band began the performance.

4. The captain walked across the lawn.

FRAME 10

Let's review what we have learned about subjects up to this point: The subject may perform the action in a sentence; sometimes the rest of the sentence describes the subject; in some sentences, the subject receives the action; the subject is often in the first part of the sentence; and a prepositional phrase seldom functions as the subject.

FRAME 11

Now let's practice what we have learned about identifying subjects.

Identify the subjects in the following sentences.

1. After quitting time, Bruce is a different person.

   _____

2. The chef was injured by the heavy pot. _____

3. The team finished its work. _____

4. Your idea is a good one. _____

5. The paper will go to the president for a signature.

   _____

FRAME 12

Sometimes there will be more than one subject in a sentence. Here are some examples of sentences with more than one subject:

1. Pie and coffee are a good lunch.
2. The apples, oranges, and pears were used to make fruit salad.
3. In the meantime, the ice cream and iced tea had grown warm.

Underline the subject in each of the above sentences.

FRAME 13

In some sentences, there are various kinds of phrases placed between the subject and verb. Do not let the existence of such phrases prevent you from finding the subject. Here are two examples:

The boss, working with his employees, developed a plan.
Ben, together with his associates, felt that the project would fail.

Note that the phrase "working with his employees" does not form an essential part of the sentence, so its omission would not greatly change the meaning of the sentence. The main part of the sentence is this: The boss developed a plan. The same pattern applies to the second example. Do not allow prepositional phrases to distract you.

Identify the subjects in the two sentences below.

1. Kevin, who moved here from Iowa, married Katy Dunn.
   _____

2. In my opinion, based on past performance, the fight will not last more than three rounds. _____

FRAME 14

This is a test to find out if you can identify subjects.

Underline the subject (or subjects) in each of the following sentences.

1. The waitress in the blue dress served bacon and eggs.

2. The typewriter was repaired by a technician.

3. The cup and saucer are the same color.

4. Eldon dropped the marbles into the jug.

5. Kenneth, drowsing in the last row, did not enjoy the play.

FRAME 15

If you correctly identified the subjects in the five sentences, then you probably have mastered the concept of identifying the subject of a sentence. If you missed any of the questions, you should go back and review. The next topic is the identification of singular and plural subjects.

FRAME 16

Subjects are plural if the form of the subject indicates more than one. Examples of plural subjects: they, we, lunches, drivers, children, kings, and nurseries. Subjects are singular if they refer to only one thing. Examples of singular subjects: he, I, lunch, driver, child, king, and nursery.

Identify the following as singular or plural.

1. creek _____

2. tax _____

3. mice _____

4. children _____

5. tables _____

FRAME 17

The subject is plural if there are two or more subjects joined by the word *and*. Example: Pencil and paper are essential tools for a writer. A subject is singular if there are two or more subjects joined by the word *or* or *nor*. Example: Either a pencil or pen is good enough.

Identify the following subjects as singular or plural.

1. Neither wind, nor rain, nor dark of night slows me down.

_____

2. Candles and matches do not give enough light.

_____

3. Neither Ken nor the cook remembers. _____

4. Jan and Betty prepared for the party. _____

FRAME 18

The next topic is the identification of verbs. A basic definition of a verb is that it expresses action or a state of being. Note the italicized examples:

Action: Harold *removed* the sign.
State of being: Betty *is* happy.

Identify the verbs in the following sentences and indicate whether each verb shows action or a state of being.

1. Peter was not happy about the problem. _____

2. Joe asked for directions. _____

3. Shorty has been sick. _____

4. Jill painted the deck with green paint. _____

FRAME 19

Both the words *has* and *been* are verbs in sentence 3 above. Verbs that occur in groups of two or three are verb phrases. Examples: has seen and shall have been.

Select the verb or verb phrase in the following sentences.

1. You have reproduced the wrong document.

2. I saw the errors at once.

3. By that time, he will have finished the project.

4. He has been considering the proposal.

FRAME 20

If you can identify the verb in a sentence, it is usually easy to find the subject of that verb. Note this example: Clarence, along with his four sons, trims the hedge along the front of the road. The one word in the sentence that shows action is the verb *trims*. Once you identify the verb, then ask: Who trims? or What trims? The answer: Clarence. Another example: One of the men is very ill. There is no action word in the example, but there is a state of being verb, *is*. Ask: Who is? The answer: One. Note that "of the men" is a prepositional phrase so it will not be the subject.

Identify the subject and verb of this sentence.

1. The leader of the band began the concert.

   subject _____ verb _____

FRAME 21

Note that the leader is the one who began. Remember that prepositional phrases are seldom the subjects of sentences. Find the verb; then find out who did the acting, if it is an action verb. If it is a state of being verb, then ask: Who is? or Who was? or Who will have been?

This is a good method to use on long, complicated sentences.

Find the subject and verb in the following sentences.

1. In most of the Ivy League colleges, selective entrance policies are the rule.

   subject _____ verb _____

2. In the National Museum in Stockholm, a famous painting shows the death of King Charles XII.

   subject _____ verb _____

3. According to the rules, as explained by Ronald, we should win easily.

   subject _____ verb _____

FRAME 22

Since identification of subject and verb is important, practice on these examples.

Select the subject and verb in each of the following sentences.

1. Ben, already an old man, complained loudly about impending fatherhood.

   subject _____ verb _____

2. The actor, along with his manager, drama coach, and hair-dresser, rented the entire suite of rooms.

   subject _____ verb _____

3. The plan of an English sentence requires a subject and verb.

   subject _____ verb _____

FRAME 23

Now that you have learned to identify subjects and verbs, you are ready for the major topic, agreement of subject and verb. The rules on agreement of subject and verb apply only to certain situations stated in the following frames.

FRAME 24

If the subject of the sentence is *I, we,* or *you,* the rule does *not* apply. The rule applies only when the sentence is in the present tense.

The next eight frames are a review of tenses. Since you just finished Chapter 7 on verb forms and tenses, you may feel certain you already know these eight frames. If so, you should move ahead to frame 33.

FRAME 25

Each verb has different forms or parts. Examples: talk, talked; know, knew, known. Different tenses require different verb forms. Tense shows when an action (or state of being) occurred. Past tense refers to action that has already happened. Examples: Yesterday I talked to Officer Jones. I finished the report late last night. He ate the entire pie.

The following sentences are all written in the past tense. Select the verb.

1. Brenda typed the letter on the old typewriter.

    _____

2. Bob drank the coffee. _____

3. We fished among the rocks. _____

FRAME 26

Present tense refers to action that is happening now; you can also use it to make statements that are generally true. Examples: He types letters with his index fingers. Bob drinks coffee with obvious enjoyment.

In the following sentences, select the verb and classify the tense as either present or past.

1. Karen works faster than her sister. _____

    _____

2. Kenneth worked hard, but he did not succeed.

    _____ _____

3. Joyce drove past here yesterday. _____

    _____

4. The cat jumped up on the table. _____

    _____

5. The dinner is ready. _____ _____

FRAME 27

The future tense refers to action that will happen in the future. The helping verb *shall* or *will* usually makes up one part of he verb. Example: He will improve. The verbs are *will* and *improve*.

Identify the two-word verb in each of the following sentences written in the future tense.

1. Betty and Leonard will prepare the lunch. _____

2. I shall return. _____

3. The psychologist will speak at 1300. _____

FRAME 28

We have discussed past, present, and future tenses; there are three additional tenses: past perfect, present perfect, and future perfect. The past perfect tense refers to action completed at some past time before some other time or event. (Reread the last sentence and think about it.) The helping verb *had* is used in the past perfect tense. Example: I had finished a second helping before Jack arrived. Note that verbs are *had* and *finished.* Also, note that the action was complete before some other event. In this case, the other event was Jack's arrival. The action completed was this: I had finished.

Identify the action completed and the other event in these sentences.

1. The cook had prepared a meal before the troops arrived.

   action completed _____ other event _____

2. I had fished in the Blue River before I left Nebraska.

   action completed _____ other event _____

FRAME 29

The present perfect tense refers to action completed before the present time. Use the helping verb *has* or *have* in the present perfect tense. The past perfect tense refers to action completed before some other event; the present perfect tense refers to action recently completed. Here is an example of present perfect tense: He has reviewed all the files.

Classify the following sentences as present perfect or past perfect.

1. I have completed the job. _____

2. I have read the entire report. _____

3. Kenneth has ruined the pudding. _____

4. She had taught them before she was married. _____

FRAME 30

The future perfect tense refers to action that will be complete at some time in the future. In the future perfect tense, there are at least three verbs—two helping verbs and the main verb. Example: By this time tomorrow, I shall have finished the project. The two helping verbs are *shall* and *have;* the main verb is *finished.* This group of three verbs is sometimes called a verb phrase.

Select the verb phrases in the following sentences.

1. On Monday, I shall have been here a year. _____

2. By noon, he will have flown his first solo flight. _____

FRAME 31

It's time to practice the identification of tenses.

Identify the tense of each of the following sentences.

1. Emory had spoken to the Army recruiter before Major Pierce arrived. _____

2. I knew that. _____

3. He will get ready for the test. _____

4. I have written the letter. _____

5. She will have created the story before she tells it. _____

6. Carl writes very well. _____

7. George has called all of the officers. _____

FRAME 32

Now we are ready to state the rule for agreement of subject and verb. The rule does not apply if the subject is *I, we,* or *you.* The rule applies only to sentences written in the present tense.

Answer the following questions about application of the rule.

1. The rule on agreement of subject and verb _____ if the subject is *I*, *we*, or *you*.

        (applies)   (does not apply)

2. The rule on agreement of subject and verb applies _____.

      (only in the present tense)   (to all tenses)

FRAME 33

The agreement rule is this: A singular subject requires a singular verb; a plural subject requires a plural verb. We have considered in some detail the singular and plural forms of subjects. In general, the singular form of verbs ends in *s*, and the plural form of verbs does *not* end in *s*. Here are some examples of singular verbs: eats, begins, knows, and thinks. Here are those same verbs in plural form: eat, begin, know, and think.

1. What kind of verbs ends in *s*? _____

FRAME 34

It may seem peculiar that the singular and plural forms of verbs form in an opposite way from nouns. However, this may be a way to help you remember each.

Complete the following table by writing the plural form of the singular verbs.

Singular	*Plural*
1. talks	_____
2. grows	_____
3. proves	_____
4. speaks	_____
5. sees	_____

FRAME 35

It is a general rule that singular verbs end in *s*. The word *singular* begins with an *s*; remember that *singular* verbs end in *s*. This rule also applies to a small group of verbs that have different internal spellings for the singular and the plural:

Singular	Plural
is	are
does	do
has	have

1. State the rule regarding the ending of singular verbs.

_____

FRAME 36

It is useful to be able to change the forms of verbs from singular to plural (and vice versa).

1. Supply the missing forms in the table below.

Singular	Plural
calls	_____
_____	go
puts	_____
_____	steal

FRAME 37

Now, let's look at an example of the application of the rule. Here it is with a singular subject and a singular verb. Example: He sings. The subject, *he*, is singular; the verb, *sings*, is also singular. Here is an example of a plural subject and a plural verb: They know about the problem. The subject, *they*, is plural; the verb, *know*, is also plural.

Underline the correct verb forms for the following sentences with singular subjects.

1. Officer Casey (review, reviews) all records.

2. He (say, says) that it was all a mistake.

3. Bob (believes, believe) all of those stories.

FRAME 38

Select the correct verb for the following sentences with plural subjects.

1. The teachers (say, says) that it is not correct.

2. The dogs (bark, barks) at the moon.

3. They (know, knows) all the answers.

4. She and I (start, starts) at 1400.

5. Henry and Tom (speak, speaks) poorly.

FRAME 39

Underline the correct verb to go with the following subjects.

1. Apples (grow, grows).

2. She (is, are).

3. Lieutenant Garman (believe, believes).

4. The cat (sleep, sleeps).

5. He (has, have).

FRAME 40

At this point, we will give you another form of the rule regarding agreement of subject and verb. If the subject is plural, then the verb will not end in *s*. Note these examples:

Plural Subjects	*Verbs*
quilts	are
boys	have
children	begin
horses	run

FRAME 41

Remember that in some sentences there are two or more subjects; such subjects are plural. Example: Ken and Kate are a happy couple. If this seems awkward, remember there are two people, Ken and Kate, and the word *they* could substitute in place of Ken and Kate. Therefore, you could write it this way: They are a happy couple.

Underline the correct verb in the following sentences that have more than one subject.

1. Ann and Barbara (believe, believes) all of the stories.

2. Beans, peas, and alfalfa (is, are) examples of legumes.

3. The patrolman and sergeant (know, knows) the procedure.

4. The book and maps (show, shows) the location of Algiers.

FRAME 42

Finally, if you forget everything else taught in this module, you should remember the two rules below. Remembering and applying these two rules will get you through a majority of situations:

1. If the subject ends in *s*, then the verb does not end in *s*.
2. If the subject does not end in *s*, then the verb will end in *s*.

QUIZ

1. Every English sentence contains a(n) _____ and _____.

2. The subject of the sentence is usually in the _____ of the sentence.

3. To make the subject agree with the verb, you must first _____ the subject.

4. Which of the following is a prepositional phrase?
   a. in the morning
   b. by myself
   c. at the end
   d. all of the above

5. True   False   A prepositional phrase seldom functions as the subject.

6. True   False   There can be more than one subject of a sentence.

7. Subjects are plural if the form of the subject indicates more than _____.

8. Which of the following is an example of a plural subject?
   a. I
   b. child
   c. we
   d. king

9. The subject is plural if two or more subjects are joined by the word _____.

10. A subject is singular if there are two or more subjects joined by the word _____ or _____.

11. A verb expresses _____ or _____ .

12. Which of the following is a verb phrase?
    a. was
    b. asked
    c. saw
    d. shall have been

13. The rule on agreement of subject and verb _____ if the subject is *I, we,* or *you.*

14. The rule on agreement of subject and verb applies only in the _____ .

15. The agreement rule is this: A singular subject requires a(n) _____; a plural subject requires a(n) _____ .

16. In general, the singular form of verbs ends in a(n) _____ .

17. In general, the plural form of verbs does _____ end in a(n) _____ .

ANSWERS TO FRAMES

Frame 2
1. subject, verb

Frame 3
1. Henry
2. Thomas Wolfe
3. dog

Frame 4
1. George
2. Margaret
3. Red Prince

Frame 5
1. A summer shower soaked Officer Williams.
2. The grass fire burned Jack.

Frame 6
1. is described
2. performs an action
3. receives action
4. performs an action

Frame 7
1. first part

Frame 9
1. As an actor
2. In his spare time
3. of the band
4. across the lawn

Frame 11
1. Bruce
2. chef

3. team
4. idea
5. paper

Frame 12

1. Pie, coffee
2. apples, oranges, pears
3. ice cream, iced tea

Frame 13

1. Kevin
2. fight

Frame 14

1. waitress
2. typewriter
3. cup, saucer
4. Eldon
5. Kenneth

Frame 16

1. singular
2. singular
3. plural
4. plural
5. plural

Frame 17

1. singular
2. plural
3. singular
4. plural

Frame 18

1. was—state of being
2. asked—action
3. has been—state of being
4. painted—action

Frame 19

1. have reproduced
2. saw
3. will have finished
4. has been considering

Frame 20

1. subject—leader   verb—began

Frame 21

1. subject—policies   verb—are
2. subject—painting   verb—shows
3. subject—we   verb—should win

Frame 22

1. subject—Ben   verb—complained
2. subject—actor   verb—rented
3. subject—plan   verb—requires

Frame 25

1. typed
2. drank
3. fished

Frame 26

1. works—present
2. worked—past
3. drove—past
4. jumped—past
5. is—present

Frame 27

1. will prepare
2. shall return
3. will speak

Frame 28

1. action completed—had prepared; other event—troops arrived.
2. action completed—had fished; other event—left Nebraska.

Frame 29

1. present perfect
2. present perfect
3. present perfect
4. past perfect

Frame 30

1. shall have been
2. will have flown

Frame 31

1. past perfect
2. past
3. future
4. present perfect

5. future perfect
6. present
7. present perfect

Frame 32
1. does not apply
2. only in the present tense

Frame 33
1. singular

Frame 34
1. talk
2. grow
3. prove
4. speak
5. see

Frame 35
1. Singular verbs end in *s*.

Frame 36

Singular	*Plural*
calls	call
goes	go
puts	put
steals	steal

Frame 37
1. reviews
2. says
3. believes

Frame 38
1. say
2. bark
3. know
4. start
5. speak

Frame 39
1. grow
2. is
3. believes
4. sleeps
5. has

Frame 41
1. believe
2. are
3. know
4. show

Capitalization

FRAME 1

This segment of the programmed learning material will teach the main rules regarding capitalization.

Most frames require a response. As in the previous chapters, you will find the correct answer at the end of each chapter. If you miss a question, go back and review the previous frame before going on.

When the instructions tell you to correct the capitalization, write lc (for lowercase) under the first letter if it is capitalized but should not be; put three lines under the first letter if it is not capitalized but should be. Note these examples.

george   **Uncle**
≡   lc

FRAME 2

The rules regarding capitalization are not especially difficult. There is one overall general rule that covers most situations. The rule is to capitalize the names of specific things but not to capitalize the names of common, or general, things.

1. _____ things usually require the use of capitals.

2. _____ things usually do not require the use of capitals.

FRAME 3

To begin, we will consider three uses of capitals *not* covered by the general rule:

1. Always capitalize the pronoun *I.*
2. Always capitalize the first word of a sentence and the first word of a line of poetry.
3. Capitalize acronyms and brevity codes.

Correct the capitalization in the following quotation.

1. "on Jordan's stormy banks i stand and cast a wishful eye to Canaan's fair and happy land where my possessions lie."

FRAME 4

The third item in frame 3 requires some additional explanation. An acronym is a word formed by the first letters of a multiword name. Example: Agency for International Development (AID). If the first letters of a multiword name do not form a word, then it is a brevity code. Examples in law enforcement: southbound (SB), in front of (IFO), gone on arrival (GOA). Note that acronyms and brevity codes require capitals. Not all abbreviations require capitals. Examples: complainant (comp), suspect (susp). In general, acronyms and brevity codes are in capitals and abbreviations in lowercase.

Which of the items below should be in lowercase? Which in capitals?

1. acronyms _____

2. abbreviations _____

3. brevity codes _____

FRAME 5

Now we will go back to the general rule. Use capitals for the names of specific people: George, Kate, Robert S. Jones. Pronouns and other words used to refer to people in general do not require capitals: they, men, mankind, she, secretary, soldier, opponent.

Correct the capitalization in the following list.

1. john carter

2. them

3. i

4. her

5. boys

6. harold

7. lieutenant green

8. captain

9. Them

FRAME 6

Note that *I* is an exception to the general rule. The capitalization rule regarding places requires the use of capitals for the names of specific places: California, Lake Michigan, Omaha, Kansas River, Norway.

Words that refer to general places do not need capitals: city, town, river, county, country, state, ocean.

When a specific name such as Pacific is combined with a general term such as ocean, then write it like this: Pacific Ocean. Other examples: Ohio River, Tulare County, New York City.

Correct the capitalization in the following list.

1. atlantic ocean

2. Creek

3. town

4. los angeles

5. sacramento river

6. gulf of mexico

7. river

8. bob's tavern

9. lake

FRAME 7

The rule holds for organizations, historical events, and documents; if you refer to a specific organization, historical event, or document, then use capital letters. Examples:

Veterans of Foreign Wars
American Revolution
Declaration of Independence.

Words that refer to general organizations, events, or documents do not require capitals. Examples: a boy's club, a rebellion, a set of bylaws.

Correct the capitalization in the following list.

1. Boy scouts

2. american legion

3. the minutes of the last meeting

4. a battle

5. battle of the Bulge

FRAME 8

Use capitals to name days of the week, months, and holidays. Note that the general terms day, month, and holiday do not require capitals. Examples: a day, but Tuesday; a month, but March; a holiday, but Christmas Day. Since the Fourth of July is a holiday, we capitalize the F in Fourth. Since the fifth of July is not a holiday, we use a small *f* in fifth.

Correct the capitalization in the following list.

1. arbor day

2. third of june

3. Monday

4. Week

5. month

FRAME 9

Use capitals for religious terms that refer to God or other words that have special religious significance. Examples: Virgin Mary, Holy Spirit, Allah. A capitalized pronoun, other than at the beginning of a sentence, probably refers to the Supreme Being. Example: I know that He is with me.

Correct the following sentence.

1. In six days God created the earth, and on the seventh day he rested.

_____

_____

FRAME 10

Use capitals to name the titles of books, plays, magazines, newspapers, articles, and poems. Examples: *War and Peace, Hair, Time, Kansas City Star,* "Psychiatric Problems Among Police Officers," "Twas the Night Before Christmas." Short words in titles such as *a, and,* and *the* do not require capitals unless they are the first word in the title.

Correct the capitalization in the following sentence.

1. The *police chief* is the magazine with the article titled "writing a comprehensive search warrant."

_____

_____

FRAME 11

Let's go back to the general rule again. Capitalize titles when used with the name of a specific person. Thus, it is correct to talk about a judge, but with the title attached to a name, it is Judge Anderson.

Correct the capitalization in the following sentence.

1. One of the presidents asked professor Jansen to arrange for an interview with chancellor Zeiss.

_____

_____

FRAME 12

When you combine common nouns with a specific name, you should use capitals for both words. Thus, street, college, creek, and company do not require capitals unless combined with specific names. Examples: Twelfth Street, Carroll College, Cripple Creek, and Ford Motor Company.

Correct the capitalization in the following sentence.

1. The stream that runs along the side of your property is Stranger creek.

_____

_____

FRAME 13

Nouns showing family relationships do not require capitals when standing alone. Examples: uncle, son, nephew.

Capitalize the relationship word when used with a specific name. Examples: Uncle Emil, Aunt Kate.

A special rule applies to father and mother. If a possessive pronoun precedes father or mother, do not use a capital; if written otherwise, use a capital. Examples:

I heard from my father.
She told Mother about the problem.

Correct the capitalization in the following sentence.

1. I know that cousin Fred will visit mother and father this summer.

_____

_____

FRAME 14

The names of directions do not usually require capitals unless they refer to a specific geographical location. Example: The North and South opposed each other in the Civil War. Another example: We drove slowly along the road that ran alternately south and then east. In the first example, North and South refer to geographical regions; in the second example, south and east refer to directions.

Correct the capitalization in the following sentence.

1. Dr. Strickland studied the history of mining in the west; he found that capital from the east financed much of the mining activity.

_____

_____

FRAME 15

Do not use capitals to name the season of the year.

Correct the capitalization in the following sentence.

1. Summer is a favorite season for many people, but Winter is the favorite season for skiers.

_____

_____

FRAME 16

Use capitals for the names of school subjects if they refer to a specific class, but do not use capitals if reference is made to a general subject. Thus, anthropology as a general subject requires no capital, but a specific class, Introduction to Anthropology, requires the use of capitals. Always use capitals to identify the names of languages. Examples: Swedish, Greek, Spanish, Hindu.

Correct the capitalization in the following sentence.

1. I had always wanted to study Geology so I registered for geology 101.

_____

_____

FRAME 17

Let's review. The first word of every sentence and the first word of a line of poetry require capitals. Always capitalize the pronoun *I*. Name specific people, places, days of the week, months, holidays, organizations, events, and documents by using capitals. Capitalize titles when combined with a proper name; common nouns combined with a proper noun require capitals. General school subjects do not require capitals; the names of specific classes require capitals. Names of languages require capitals. Do not use capitals for names of seasons. Do not capitalize the names of directions unless they refer to a specific region.

References to God and other important religious references require capitalization.

FRAME 18

Correct the following list of items so that the capitalization is correct.

1. Robert Carl _____

2. Jenny _____

3. world war ii _____

4. thursday _____

5. March _____

6. *the red badge of courage* _____

7. king Charles _____

8. summer _____

9. Fifth avenue _____

10. uncle Oliver _____

11. Newsweek _____

QUIZ

1. There is one overall general rule that covers most spelling situations. This is to capitalize:
   a. specific things.
   b. common things.
   c. general things.
   d. none of the above.

2. Always capitalize the pronoun _____.

3. Always capitalize the _____ word of a sentence.

4. Which of the following is correct?
   a. c.i.a.
   b. n.b.c.
   c. c.b.s.
   d. ABC

5. Which of the following is correct?
   a. City
   b. River
   c. California
   d. County

6. Which of the following is correct?
   a. tuesday
   b. March
   c. fourth of july
   d. christmas day

7. Which of the following is correct?
   a. *huckleberry finn*
   b. *a street car named desire*
   c. *Los Angeles Times*
   d. "twinkle, twinkle little star"

8. Capitalize titles when used with the name of a(n) _____.

9. Capitalize a relationship word when used with a(n) _____.

10. Which of the following is correct?
    a. Officer Smith drove southbound on Church Street.
    b. The East played the West in the Shrine Game.
    c. The North and the South opposed each other in the Civil War.
    d. All of the above are correct.

11. Which of the following is correct?
    a. Summer is my favorite season.
    b. In the winter, I go skiing.
    c. I love April because it is the beginning of spring.
    d. All of the above are correct.

12. Which of the following is correct?
    a. I think Anthropology is a fascinating subject.
    b. I took Philosophy 101 last semester.
    c. I would like to learn spanish.
    d. I have learned to appreciate english much better.

ANSWERS TO FRAMES

Frame 2
1. Specific
2. General (or common)

Frame 3
1. On   I

Frame 4
1. capitals
2. lowercase
3. capitals

Frame 5
1. John Carter
3. I
6. Harold
7. Lieutenant Green
9. them

Frame 6
1. Atlantic Ocean
2. Creek
4. Los Angeles
5. Sacramento River
6. Gulf of Mexico
8. Bob's Tavern

Frame 7
1. Boy Scouts
2. American Legion
5. Battle of the Bulge

Frame 8
1. Arbor Day
2. third of June
4. week

Frame 9
1. He

Frame 10
1. *Police Chief* "Writing a Comprehensive Search Warrant"

Frame 11
1. Professor   Chancellor

Frame 12
1. Creek

Frame 13
1. Cousin Fred   Mother   Father

Frame 14

1. West   East

Frame 15

1. winter

Frame 16

1. geology   Geology 101

Frame 18

1. correct
2. correct
3. World War II

4. Thursday
5. correct
6. *The Red Badge of Courage*
7. King Charles
8. correct
9. Fifth Avenue
10. Uncle Oliver
11. correct

10

Punctuation

FRAME 1

This segment of programmed learning material will teach some of the important rules about punctuation. This segment teaches end punctuation and the use of various punctuation marks. The next chapter on punctuation teaches the internal punctuation of sentences.

Most frames require a response; you will find the correct answer at the end of this chapter. If you miss a question, go back and review the previous frame before going on.

FRAME 2

The responses to this programmed material will often be a correctly placed punctuation mark. To show the correct placement, write the word preceding the punctuation mark and the punctuation. Note the examples below.

Nature of Response	*Looks Like This*
Show placement of comma	king,
Show that no punctuation is needed	there
Show italics	<u>Wuthering Heights</u>
Show placement of hyphen	one-eight

FRAME 3

The period is the first of the punctuation marks we shall consider. Here are two common uses. It can show the end of a sentence; sometimes we find it after an abbreviation.

1. Name two uses of a period.

_____

_____

FRAME 4

A period always marks the end of a sentence. This use of a period rarely creates a problem. The question of whether or not to use a period after an abbreviation is difficult to answer. The general rule is to use a period after an abbreviation, but not after an acronym or after a brevity code. There are exceptions to the rule; if in doubt, consult a dictionary.

As a general rule, which of the following requires a period? (answer yes or no)

1. Abbreviation _____

2. Acronym _____

3. Brevity code _____

FRAME 5

Three periods with space between make a punctuation mark called the ellipsis (. . .). The ellipsis shows an omission in quoted material. Example: "The economy is making a full recovery . . . ; we expect full employment by this time next year." The ellipsis shows the omission of the phrase "even though interest rates are troublesome."

1. A set of three periods used to show an omission in quoted material is called a(n) _____.

FRAME 6

Use the question mark after a direct question that requests information. Examples: Is the dog in the house? Is Sergeant Moore on duty today? Do *not* use a question mark after an indirect question. Example: He wanted to know how I had found it.

Select the correct punctuation for these sentences.

1. Will you please return my book (period or question mark)

2. Is this the correct report form for this crime (period or question mark)

3. Lieutenant Brooks asked if our uniforms were clean (period or question mark)

FRAME 7

Use the exclamation mark after a word, phrase, or sentence that indicates strong emotion. Use it sparingly because it has little place in police and correctional report writing.

The exclamation mark, question mark, and period are all end punctuation marks.

1. The three kinds of end punctuation are _____,
   _____, and _____.

FRAME 8

The apostrophe is the next punctuation mark for consideration. One of the uses of an apostrophe is to show possession of nouns; it also shows possession of pronouns other than personal pronouns. If you want to form the possessive of a noun that does not end in the letter *s*, add an apostrophe and an *s*. This applies to singular nouns and to some plurals that do not end in *s* such as men or children.

Noun	*Possessive Form*
boy	boy's
cat	cat's
men	men's

Form the possessive of these words.

1. someone _____

2. women _____

3. Hank _____

FRAME 9

If you want to form the possessive of a word that ends in *s*, then you add an apostrophe and the letter *s*; this is the same rule previously discussed. But if a noun ends in *s*, there are exceptions to the rule. One exception: If adding an apostrophe and an *s* makes pronunciation difficult, then you simply add an apostrophe.

This creates no pronunciation problem:	James's plans
This would create a problem:	Socrates's discussions
So add only an apostrophe:	Socrates' discussions

Select the phrases that are correctly punctuated.

1. Lois' talk *or* Lois's talk

2. Moses' writings *or* Moses's writings

FRAME 10

The plural of most nouns ends in *s;* form the possessive of plurals ending in *s* by adding an apostrophe to the final *s.* Examples:

> police officers' riot gear
> correctional officers' training room
> Commission on Peace Officers' Standards and Training

Use the rules on the use of apostrophes to correctly punctuate the following phrases.

1. Pete's apple *or* Petes' apple

2. the four boy's house *or* the four boys' house

3. women's work *or* womens' work

4. Titus's book *or* Titus' book

FRAME 11

In a compound word, make the last word possessive. Examples: mother-in-law's cake (singular possessive), attorneys-general's presentation (plural possessive), attorney-general's presentation (singular possessive).

Use the rules on apostrophes and possession to correctly punctuate the following phrases.

1. a (bachelors *or* bachelor's *or* bachelors') pad

2. the two (brothers-in-law's *or* brothers-in-laws') cars

3. Aristophanes' plays *or* Aristophanes's plays

FRAME 12

If two (or more) nouns are owners of something, then the noun closer (or closest) shows the possession. Example: Dick and Bob's garden. The example shows joint possession of one garden. Example to show that each had a garden: Dick's and Bob's gardens.

Use the rules on apostrophes and possession to correctly punctuate the following.

1. We borrowed the (children's *or* childrens') game.

2. We saw (Betty *or* Betty's) and Jan's house.

3. Is this (Lewis' *or* Lewis's) work?

FRAME 13

Let us review. If a word does not end in *s*, then add an apostrophe and the letter *s* to make the possessive form. If the word is singular and ends in *s*, add an apostrophe and the letter *s* unless this makes pronunciation difficult; in that case, add only an apostrophe. When the plural of a word ends in *s* (most do), add only an apostrophe to form the plural possessive. In compounds, possession is shown by the last word of the compound. To show joint possession, make only the last noun possessive; to show individual possession, make all the nouns possessive.

FRAME 14

If you want to show possession by an inanimate object, do it by constructing a prepositional phrase. Do not write "a chair's leg"; instead, follow the style of these examples: the leg of the chair, the branches of the tree, the spokes of the wheel. "The horse's ear" and "the bull's horns" are correct usages.

Underline the correct usage between the given pairs.

1. book's page *or* page of the book

2. cat's paw *or* paw of the cat

3. week's last day *or* last day of the week

FRAME 15

There is a place where you should not use an apostrophe: Do *not* use it to show possession of personal pronouns such as his, hers, theirs, ours, and its. Personal pronouns change form to show possession and do not require the use of apostrophes. *Its* is the possessive form of *it*. *Its* is sometimes confused with *it's*, which is a contraction for *it is*.

Underline the correct punctuation in these sentences.

1. That umbrella is (hers, her's).

2. (It's, Its) a good day for a picnic.

FRAME 16

The apostrophe has uses other than that of showing possession. An apostrophe can show omission of letters and numbers:

'18 = 1918
can't = can not

don't = do not
it's = it is
they're = they are

FRAME 17

The apostrophe also shows the plurals of letters and numbers. Examples:

There are seven *r*'s in the sentence.
He makes his 9's to look like 7's.

Correctly punctuate the following sentence.

1. Don't forget to dot your i s and cross your t s.

FRAME 18

Hyphens are the next punctuation to consider. They have a number of uses, but not many that cause problems. Hyphens show the continuation of a word from one line to the next. Consult a dictionary to find out how to divide a word.

Use hyphens to form compound numbers from twenty-one through ninety-nine. Use them to separate the numerator from the denominator in written fractions. Examples: one-fourth, three-fifths.

Change these numbers to written word form using hyphens as needed.

1. 1/8 _____

2. 2/3 _____

3. 34 _____

Note: Numbers should never be used to begin a sentence. Always write a number that begins a sentence. Example: One-eighth of the class failed (*not* 1/8th of the class failed).

FRAME 19

Use the hyphen after the prefixes *ex-, anti-, self-,* and *all-* and before the suffix *-elect.* Examples: self-administered, ex-wife, all-state, governor-elect. There are enough exceptions to this rule that it will pay to do some checking in the dictionary.

Review the following and correct any errors in the use of hyphens.

1. John Starr is now mayor elect since he won by a three fifths majority.

2. Sports writers selected Peter to the all metro team.

3. Nebraska won by a score of forty four to seven.

FRAME 20

Use a hyphen to join two or more words that serve as a single adjective before a noun. Examples: semi-skilled labor, well-known speaker.

Review the following and correct any errors in the use of hyphens.

1. Margaret was wearing a blue green dress.

2. The paragraph contained seventy eight words.

3. Senator elect Stewart spoke at the rally.

FRAME 21

Do *not* use a hyphen between chemical compounds, certain governmental positions, and words showing military rank. Examples: sodium chloride, lieutenant governor, lieutenant colonel.

Review the following and correct any errors in the use of hyphens.

1. We waited for the President elect to come down and speak to us.

2. Brigadier-General Mason lives in quarters on Grant Avenue.

3. Ask Sergeant-Major Briggs about the two thirds rule.

FRAME 22

Use the hyphen to form compound words. The compound usually combines two or more words, with different functions and qualities, to indicate a single idea. Examples: secretary-treasurer, brother-in-law, do-it-yourselfer. When several words combine to make a single idea, the hyphen is often appropriate. Since there is no rule, consult a dictionary.

FRAME 23

The dash differs from a hyphen in that it is twice as long as a hyphen. Most typed copy shows a dash by putting two hyphens together like this: --. A common use of the dash is to show an interruption or abrupt change of thought in the middle of a sentence. Example: In 1968—I was only 24 years old—my unit was sent to Vietnam.

Show the correct use of dashes in the following sentences.

1. The mayor a former police officer with the city of Los Angeles has always lived in Los Angeles.

2. Officer Johnson tall, serious, and lean seemed to be the perfect candidate for police work.

FRAME 24

Sometimes a dash helps to make the meaning clear. Note these examples:

> Three patients, Wilson, Bryan, and Carter, were in the waiting room.
> Three patients—Wilson, Bryan, and Carter—were in the waiting room.

In the first example, you may be led to believe that six people are in the waiting room. In the second example, it is clear that there are only three people in the waiting room.

Show the correct use of dashes in the following sentence.

1. The old guard, Bob Peterson, Harry West, and Phil Kearney, were ready for the campaign.

FRAME 25

Some people use the dash as a substitute for other forms of punctuation. Use the dash sparingly if you understand its use. Do not use it at all unless you are sure you are correct.

FRAME 26

Quotation marks have a variety of uses; the most common use is to enclose a direct quotation from either a written or a spoken source. Example: The squad sergeant said, "Fall in on this line." The quotation marks show an exact quote; they are not correct for indirect quotations such as this: The squad sergeant told us to fall in on the white line. Note that there is a comma before the quotation mark; the end punctuation, a period, is inside the quotation mark.

Correctly place quotation marks, if needed, in the following sentence.

1. Mary called for the children to come home.

FRAME 27

There are quotation marks (") and single quotation marks ('). The single quotation mark shows a quote within a quote. Example: Byron said, "Remember Captain Field's motto, 'Never run when you can walk.' "

Correctly place quotation marks, if needed, in the following sentence.

1. Senator Johnson said, Remember the advice of Teddy Roosevelt who said, Speak softly and carry a big stick.

FRAME 28

Quotation marks have other uses. They set off titles of poems, songs, articles, and short stories, but not book-length materials. Example: Emerson wrote "Concord Hymn" to commemorate the battles of Lexington and Concord.

Correctly place quotation marks, if needed, in the following sentence.

1. Robert Frost wrote numerous poems such as Mending Wall and Death of the Hired Man.

FRAME 29

Words used in a special sense are set off by quotation marks to show a special meaning. Example: Casey was wearing his "new" hat. The quotation marks enclosing the word *new* may indicate that the hat is not really new. Another example: In among the clutter of hubcaps, broken chrome strips, and old radiators, the "artist" was creating a "masterpiece." Here the quotation marks show an unconventional concept of both artist and masterpiece.

Correctly place quotation marks to show a special meaning in the following sentences.

1. Pursuit driving is section J-6 of the General Orders Manual.

2. As far as Woody was concerned, every Monday was a holiday.

3. Because Officer Harris has red hair and is a very large officer, he is known on his beat as Big Red.

FRAME 30

The comma is the next punctuation mark we will consider. Writers use this punctuation mark frequently, but they often use it incorrectly. There is a discussion of the use of the comma for punctuating internal clauses and phrases in Chapter 11, Internal Punctuation. The first use of the comma we will cover is its use in direct address. When you directly address a person by name, you use a comma after the person's name. Examples:

> Allen, will you please turn in the shotguns?
> Yes, Peter, we do have to take a report.

Show the placement of commas in the following sentence.

1. Charles please make sure you pay for our meals.

FRAME 31

A very common use of the comma is to separate three or more items in a series. Example: Each night before my patrol shift, I make sure I have my baton, handcuffs, briefcase, and penal code.

Correctly place commas in the following sentence.

1. Show the visitors the china old guns antique chair and old books.

FRAME 32

Sometimes items within a series will contain commas; in that case, use a semicolon to separate items in a series. Example: I went shopping and bought the following things: shoes, gloves, and a scarf for my wife; cigars, socks, and a hat for Daniel; and a bicycle, skates, and a sled for Bobby.

Correctly place commas and semicolons in the following sentence.

1. To get ready to move we did these things: cleaned the basement garage and stairs packed the glasses cups and silver and removed the shelves.

FRAME 33

Let us return to commas again. Use a comma to separate coordinate adjectives. Adjectives are coordinate if each adjective separately modifies the noun. Example: He is an energetic, happy dog. Not all adjectives are coordinate. Example: The cabin is next to a large dead tree. It is possible to reverse coordinate adjectives: happy, energetic dog. The word *and* can substitute for the comma if the adjectives are coordinate. If in doubt as to whether adjectives are coordinate and require a comma, substitute the word *and* for the comma and see if it makes sense. If so, use a comma. Try this test on these sentences and show correct punctuation.

1. He worked only at simple boring jobs.

2. You should stop at the new hardware store.

FRAME 34

The comma marks the end of unquoted material before beginning a quotation. Example: The sergeant appeared at the crime scene and shouted, "Jones and O'Malley, get over here and secure the scene."

Place the comma correctly in the following sentence.

1. I always remember what George said "Show bettors never make money."

FRAME 35

Use the comma in the following situations:

- Addresses such as this: Modesto, California
- Salutation of a personal letter: Dear Jane,
- Closing of a letter: Sincerely, *or* Yours truly,

FRAME 36

Use the rules in frame 35 to correctly punctuate the following.

Dear Bob   March 10 2003

I have moved to San Diego California

                                                                        Sincerely

                                                                        Jim

FRAME 37

Another use of the comma is to set off an appositive. An appositive placed next to a noun or pronoun explains the noun or pronoun by renaming it. Examples:

Henry Case, the electrician, is here to fix the pump.
He sent the book to Dr. John Sayles, Dean of the Teachers College.

Correctly place commas in these sentences.

1. The veteran Officer Robert Sass was respected by all of the members of the squad.

2. Warden Paul Gleason a former Olympic wrestler talked to the correctional officers.

FRAME 38

The colon is the next punctuation mark for consideration. A common use of the colon is to introduce a list. Example: Karl is an expert at certain sports such as the following: ice hockey, softball, and swimming. Do *not* use the colon after verbs such as *are.* Example of incorrect use: Common problems are: a lack of money, intemperance, and noise.

Correctly place colons, if needed, in the following sentences.

1. In college I took courses such as the following English, sociology, geography, and psychology.

2. On the shelf there are wheels, nuts, bolts, and washers.

FRAME 39

You can use the colon as the grammatical equivalent of an equal sign. Example: Many of our social and economic problems have been caused by the failure of a single entity: the American family.

Correctly place a colon, if needed, in the following sentence.

1. The consequences of the extensive drought were inevitable famine and many deaths.

FRAME 40

Use the colon after the salutation of a formal letter:

Dear Chief Williams:

FRAME 41

Use the rules regarding the use of colons to correctly punctuate the following.

1. Dear Warden Van Alst

2. Dear Barbara

3. Buy these things a pencil, towel, and toothbrush.

FRAME 42

Italics are a special kind of type used in printed work. In hand-written and typewritten copy, writers are not able to supply italics so they provide italics by <u>underlining</u>. Italicize the names of books, newspapers, and magazines. Remember to set off titles of articles, chapters, poems, etc., in quotation marks. Note the following example: There is an article in *Police Chief* entitled "Forensic Hypnosis and Investigation."

Correctly punctuate the following sentence.

1. The first chapter in Statistical Analysis in Psychology and Education is titled Basic Ideas in Statistics.

FRAME 43

The names of ships and aircraft, titles of works of art, movies, television programs, radio programs, and record albums require italics.

Use the rules of italics to correct the following sentence.

1. Last night I read the Fresno Bee and watched Seinfeld.

FRAME 44

Italics identify foreign words and phrases. Example: In the criminal law class, the professor used the term *ex post facto* laws, but Walter did not understand what he meant.

Correct the following sentence.

1. The professor explained that the corpus delicti is the same as the elements of the crime.

FRAME 45

This frame is a review test of punctuation.

1. What punctuation mark shows omission of part of some quoted material? _____

Name the three end punctuation marks.

2. _____

3. _____

4. _____

Show the correct punctuation for the following sentences.

5. The cats paw was bleeding.

6. The four officers jobs changed.

7. I wish you would make your 5s differently.

8. We were there for twenty nine days

9. Richard said, I did all of that yesterday.

10. The soprano sang Abide With Me.

11. Pete will you please stop at my desk

12. She lives in Waukegan Illinois.

13. He talked to these people Mary, Janet, Sandra, and Betty.

14. He claimed to have read War and Peace in one day.

QUIZ

1. A set of three periods used to show an omission in quoted material is called a(n)_____.

2. Use the hyphen after the prefixes _____, _____, _____, and _____ and before the suffix _____.

3. Use a(n) _____ to join two or more words that serve as a single adjective before a noun.

4. Which of the following is a correct use of a hyphen?
   a. He is an ex-police officer.
   b. Brigadier-General Jackson was known as "Stonewall."
   c. Sulfuric-acid is hazardous.
   d. Lieutenant-Governor Davis is running for governor.

5. Use the hyphen to form _____ words.

6. Which of the following is correct?
   a. secretary-treasurer
   b. father-in-law
   c. do-it-yourselfer
   d. pie-in-the-sky attitude
   e. all of the above

7. True   False   The dash (—) is used to show an interruption or abrupt change of thought in the middle of a sentence.

8. The most common use of quotation marks is:
   a. to set off titles of poems, songs, articles, and short stories.
   b. to enclose a direct quotation from either a written or a spoken source.
   c. Neither is more common than the other.

9. Italics or underlining should be used with:
   a. books.
   b. newspapers.
   c. magazines.
   d. all of the above.

10. Other applications of italics are the names of _____ and _____, _____, movies, _____, _____, radio programs, and _____.

11. Which of the following is the proper use of italics or underlining?
    a. The professor talked about ex post facto laws.
    b. John asked me to help him get elected, and there would be a quid pro quo.
    c. Whistler's Mother is a famous work of art.
    d. Yellow Submarine is a famous Beatles' album.

ANSWERS TO FRAMES

Frame 3
1. to end a sentence
2. sometimes used in abbreviations

Frame 4
1. yes
2. no
3. no

Frame 5
1. ellipsis

Frame 6
1. period
2. question mark
3. period

Frame 7
1. period   question mark   exclamation mark

Frame 8
1. someone's

2. women's
3. Hank's

Frame 9

1. Lois's talk
2. Moses' writings

Frame 10

1. Pete's apple
2. boys' house
3. women's work
4. Titus's book

Frame 11

1. bachelor's
2. brothers-in-law's cars
3. Aristophanes' plays

Frame 12

1. children's
2. Betty
3. Lewis's

Frame 14

1. page of the book
2. cat's paw
3. last day of the week

Frame 15

1. hers
2. It's

Frame 17

1. i's   t's

Frame 18

1. one-eighth
2. two-thirds
3. thirty-four

Frame 19

1. mayor-elect; three-fifths
2. all-metro
3. forty-four

Frame 20

1. blue-green

2. seventy-eight
3. Senator-elect

Frame 21

1. President-elect
2. Brigadier General
3. Sergeant Major; two-thirds

Frame 23

1. mayor—   Los Angeles—
2. Johnson—   lean—

Frame 24

1. guard—   Phil Kearney—

Frame 26

1. no quotation marks needed

Frame 27

1. said, "Remember said,
   'Speak   stick.' "

Frame 28

1. "Mending Wall"   "Death of the
   Hired Man."

Frame 29

1. "Pursuit driving"
2. "holiday."
3. "Big Red."

Frame 30

1. Charles,

Frame 31

1. china,   guns,   chair,

Frame 32

1. basement,   garage,   stairs;
   glasses,   cups,   silver;

Frame 33

1. simple,
2. new

Frame 34

1. said,

Frame 36

1. Bob,   10,   San Diego,   Sincerely,

Frame 37

1. veteran, Sass,
2. Gleason, wrestler,

Frame 38

1. following:
2. no colon needed

Frame 39

1. inevitable:

Frame 41

1. Van Alst:
2. Barbara,
3. things:

Frame 42

1. Statistical Analysis in Psychology and Education "Basic Ideas in Statistics."

Frame 43

1. Fresno Bee
   Seinfeld

Frame 44

1. corpus delicti

Frame 45

1. ellipsis (. . .)
2. period
3. question mark
4. exclamation mark
5. cat's
6. officers'
7. 5's
8. twenty-nine
9. said, "I . . . yesterday."
10. "Abide With Me."
11. Pete,
12. Waukegan,
13. people:
14. War and Peace

11

Internal Punctuation

FRAME 1

This segment of programmed learning material will teach the rules regarding the internal punctuation of phrases and clauses.

Most frames require a response. You will find the correct answer at the end of this chapter. If you miss a question, go back and review the previous frame before going on.

FRAME 2

We will begin the instruction on internal punctuation by learning about phrases and several kinds of clauses. A clause contains a subject and verb. We can classify clauses as either main or subordinate. A main clause can stand alone as a complete sentence, but a subordinate clause cannot stand alone.

Complete this sentence.

1. A clause contains a subject and verb; clauses are either _____ or _____.

FRAME 3

Another name for a main clause is independent clause; another name for subordinate clause is dependent clause. Here is an example of a sentence containing both kinds of clauses: Although the sun was shining, the humidity made the day uncomfortable. The clause "Although the sun was shining" cannot stand alone as a complete sentence so it is a dependent clause. The other clause, "the humidity made the day uncomfortable," can stand alone so it is an independent clause.

1. A(n) _____ clause can stand alone as a sentence.

2. A(n) _____ clause cannot stand alone as sentence.

FRAME 4

Dependent clauses usually begin with words such as these: if, when, while, as, although. Dependent clauses are subordinate to the main clause; the main clause or independent clause carries the main idea, and the subordinate clause adds to the main idea. Example: While the scouts slept, the scoutmaster prepared plans for the next day. The main idea concerns the scoutmaster; the idea about scouts sleeping is subordinate.

Underline the dependent clause in this sentence.

1. If Chris can get his car fixed, we will leave tomorrow.

FRAME 5

A sentence may contain one of each kind of clause, or it may have one independent clause and two or three dependent clauses; other combinations are also possible. Note that the previous sentence contains three independent clauses; each could stand alone.

Classify each of the five clauses in the following example. Letters in parentheses show the end of each clause.

1. If Mac receives the shipment on time, (a) he will complete the project; (b) if the shipment is delayed, (c) the boss will fire several people (d) and the project will be finished later. (e)

   independent _____

   dependent _____

FRAME 6

A phrase is a group of related words that does *not* have both subject and verb. The prepositional phrase is probably the most common kind of phrase. Examples: in your room, by myself, at the end, on the bottom. In the examples, the first word in each phrase is a preposition; the last word in each phrase is a noun or pronoun.

1. A group of words that contains both subject and verb is a(n) _____.

2. A group of related words without both subject and verb is a(n) _____.

FRAME 7

Now we shall consider the punctuation of phrases. Many phrases do not require punctuation. Example: At the post office I bought stamps and got mail. Sometimes a comma helps to make the meaning clear. Example: On the first green, golfers are confident. Unless a comma is placed after "green," it might appear to say that golfers are green. Phrases that are very long may require punctuation with a comma. State which (if any) of the following phrases require punctuation.

1. In winter we stay inside. _____

2. In 1972 my salary was adequate. _____

3. On the count of three move out quickly. _____

FRAME 8

In most sentences the writer should not punctuate prepositional phrases. If in doubt, do not punctuate. Try to keep your writing free from unnecessary punctuation. Phrases at the beginning of a sentence seldom require punctuation; phrases at the end of a sentence almost never require punctuation. State which (if any) of the following phrases require punctuation.

1. All of the members of the group were looking for the secretary.

_____

2. At the time Harold was waiting in the waiting room.

_____

FRAME 9

Clauses, on the other hand, often require punctuation. Consider this example, which consists of two independent clauses: Casey opened the gifts, I picked up the paper and string. The example contains a major error in punctuation. Do *not* connect two independent clauses with a comma. Such an error is a comma splice.

Answer the following two questions regarding the use of commas.

1. Two independent clauses (may, may not) be connected by a comma.

2. Connecting two independent clauses with a comma is called a(n) _____.

FRAME 10

There are several ways to connect independent clauses:

1. A conjunction such as *and* can connect the clauses: Casey opened the gifts, and I picked up the paper and string.
2. A semicolon can connect the clauses: Casey opened the gifts; I picked up the paper and string.
3. If one of the clauses changes to a dependent clause, a comma can connect the clauses: While I picked up the paper and string, Casey opened the gifts.

Note: In the third example, adding the word *while* makes that clause dependent.

1. Which of these—colon, semicolon, comma—can connect two independent clauses? _____

FRAME 11

Sometimes a semicolon and a conjunctive adverb connect independent clauses. Example: John continued to study piano; however, I no longer paid for the lessons. The words *however* and *indeed, consequently,* and *moreover* are all conjunctive adverbs. Correct punctuation requires placement of a semicolon before the conjunctive adverb and a comma after it.

Select the correct punctuation for the following sentence.

1. Harry was my best customer consequently he received preferential treatment.

FRAME 12

When a dependent clause begins a sentence, a comma sets it off from the rest of the sentence. The previous sentence is an example. If the independent clause comes first, a comma may not be necessary. Example: We shall finish the project if Harold provides the material. There is no rule as to whether to use a comma when the dependent clause comes after the independent clause. Use a comma if it improves the sentence.

Select the correct punctuation for the following sentence.

   1. Joseph repaired transmissions if he had time.

FRAME 13

Next, we shall learn about restrictive and nonrestrictive clauses. A nonrestrictive element is a word or group of words that provides additional, but not critical, information about the word or words that it modifies. Omitting a nonrestrictive element will not greatly change the meaning of the sentence. Restrictive elements restrict, or greatly change, whatever they modify.

   1. A word or group of words that provides useful, but not critical, information is a(n) _____ element.

FRAME 14

Here are some examples; underlining identifies the restrictive or nonrestrictive element. Restrictive: A boss <u>who is fair</u> will be popular with employees. Nonrestrictive: John Spencer, <u>who has a full beard</u>, arrived at the barbershop. The second group of words does little to change the meaning of the sentence; hence, it is nonrestrictive. To test if an element is restrictive, say the sentence with the element omitted. If the meaning of the sentence does not change or changes only slightly, then it is probably nonrestrictive. Try the test on the underlined portion of the following sentence and label it as restrictive or nonrestrictive.

   1. That is the book <u>that was responsible for the war.</u>
     _____

FRAME 15

Classify the following elements as restrictive or nonrestrictive. The places marked (x) may or may not contain missing punctuation.

   1. Kathy Barrett (x) an attorney from Tulsa (x) handled the case for the plaintiff. _____

   2. Kathy Barrett (x) is an attorney from Tulsa. _____

3. Kathy Barrett (x) who is the best attorney in the Midwest (x) will handle the case.

_____

FRAME 16

In frame 15 it is possible to punctuate sentence 3 either way. If you insert commas, then "will handle the case" is the more important part. If "who is the best attorney in the Midwest" is more important, then omit the commas.

1. Use commas to enclose _____ elements.

2. Do not use commas for _____ elements.

FRAME 17

Closely related to the nonrestrictive element is the parenthetical expression, which is a group of words that interrupts the sentence and changes the meaning hardly at all. Example: Police officers, and firemen too, have jobs that are very stressful at times. The parenthetical expression is "and firemen too."

Classify these sentences as having nonrestrictive or parenthetical elements.

1. Betty, who has blond hair, looked especially good in her brown dress. _____

2. Harry Porter, you remember, was in town yesterday.

_____

FRAME 18

This frame is a review test of internal punctuation.

1. A group of words that has both subject and verb is a(n) _____.

2. A group of related words that does not have a subject and verb is a(n) _____.

Show the correct punctuation for the following sentences.

3. There are strange noises the child is afraid to go to sleep.

4. If he doesn't call by noon go ahead without him.

5. Peter Zook a former police sergeant got the California P.O.S.T. consultant position.

QUIZ

1. A clause contains a(n) _____ and a(n) _____.

2. A clause is classified as either _____ or _____; these clauses are also known as _____ and _____ clauses.

3. A(n) _____ can stand alone as a sentence.

4. A(n) _____ cannot stand alone as a sentence.

5. Which of the following can begin a dependent clause?
   a. if
   b. when
   c. while
   d. as
   e. although
   f. all of the above

6. True   False   There can be only one independent and one dependent clause in any sentence.

7. True   False   A phrase is a group of related words that has both a subject and verb.

8. The punctuation most often used with phrases is a:
   a. comma.
   b. period.
   c. semicolon.
   d. colon.

9. True   False   In most sentences the writer should not punctuate prepositional phrases.

10. True   False   Two independent clauses should be connected with a comma.

11. Connecting two independent clauses with a comma is an error called a(n) _____.

12. Two independent clauses can be connected by which of the following punctuation?
   a. and
   b. semicolon

    c. conjunctive adverb
    d. all of the above

13. Which of the following are conjunctive adverbs?
    a. however
    b. indeed
    c. consequently
    d. moreover
    e. all of the above

14. If a dependent clause begins a sentence, a(n) _____ sets it off from the rest of the sentence.

15. A word or group of words that provides useful, but not critical, information is a(n) _____ element.

16. True   False   Nonrestrictive elements are set off with commas.

17. A parenthetical expression is a group of words that _____ _____ _____ but changes the meaning barely at all.

ANSWERS TO FRAMES

Frame 2
1. main, subordinate (or vice versa)

Frame 3
1. main or independent
2. subordinate or dependent

Frame 4
1. <u>If Chris can get his car fixed,</u>

Frame 5
1. independent: b, d, e
   dependent: a, c

Frame 6
1. clause
2. phrase

Frame 7
1. not required
2. not required
3. required

Frame 8
1. not required
2. not required

Frame 9
1. may not
2. comma splice

Frame 10
1. semicolon

Frame 11
1. customer;   consequently,

Frame 12
1. no punctuation needed

Frame 13
1. nonrestrictive

Frame 14
1. restrictive

Frame 15

1. nonrestrictive
2. restrictive
3. nonrestrictive or restrictive (see following discussion)

Frame 16

1. nonrestrictive
2. restrictive

Frame 17

1. nonrestrictive
2. parenthetical

Frame 18

1. clause
2. phrase
3. noises;
4. noon,
5. Zook, sergeant,

Adjectives and Adverbs

FRAME 1

This segment of programmed learning material will help you avoid errors in the use of adjectives and adverbs.

Most frames require a response; the correct answer is available at the end of the chapter. If you miss a question, go back and review the previous frame before going on.

FRAME 2

In order to avoid errors in the use of adjectives and adverbs, it is first necessary to be able to identify adjectives and adverbs. Both adjectives and adverbs are modifiers; they change or adjust the meaning of other words.

1. Both adjectives and adverbs are _____.

FRAME 3

An adjective is a word that modifies or describes a noun or its equivalent. Articles—words such as *a, an,* and *the*—are a special type of adjective. In the examples below, underlining identifies the adjectives:

> a <u>slow</u> pitch
> <u>old</u> table
> the <u>tired</u> tiger

Underline the adjectives in the following sentence.

1. We gave the president a substantial raise.

FRAME 4

Let's go into more detail about adjectives. They describe or limit nouns or noun substitutes. Adjectives show degrees of comparison. Examples: big, bigger, biggest; slow, slower, slowest; good, better, best. In most sentences you will find the adjectives placed just before the noun. Examples: white socks, green table. A predicate adjective does not precede the noun it modifies. Example: Her hair is beautiful. In the example, "beautiful" is a predicate adjective modifying "hair."

Underline the predicate adjectives in the following sentences.

1. Henry's lectures are tiresome.

2. After a winter in the city, David's face was pale.

FRAME 5

An adverb is a word that modifies a verb, an adjective, or another adverb. Adverbs often end in -ly. In the examples below, underlining identifies the adverbs:

He learns quickly. (modifies a verb)
He is very shy. (modifies an adjective)
He did it quite easily. (modifies another adverb)

Underline the adverbs in the following sentence.

1. Jake opened the valve very carefully.

FRAME 6

Here is some more information about adverbs. As previously noted, many adverbs end in -ly. They also answer the questions where, how, when, why, to what degree, and true or false. Note these examples:

where	inside, outside
how	slowly, carefully
when	soon, never
why	consequently, therefore
to what degree	completely, partially
true or false	not, surely

Some adjectives can change to adverbs by adding -ly. Examples: slow, slowly; rapid, rapidly.

FRAME 7

Both adjectives and adverbs are modifiers; it is important to know which words they modify. Consider this example: John sings sweetly in the red tub.

Modifier	*Word Modified*
sweetly	sings
the, red	tub

In this example the adverb follows the verb and the adjectives precede the noun; this is a common pattern.

Make a table like the one above using the following sentence.

She worked carelessly and made several mistakes.

Modifier	*Word Modified*
_____	_____
_____	_____

FRAME 8

Sometimes it is tricky to identify the modifier and the word modified. Consider this example: He opened the door very slowly. In the example the adverb "very" modifies another adverb, "slowly"; "slowly" modifies the verb "opened" at the other end of the sentence. In the following sentence, identify the adverb and the verb it modifies.

1. The police ordinance expert defused the bomb carefully.

_____

FRAME 9

Remember that adjectives can only modify nouns or their equivalents; they cannot modify a verb. Therefore it is not correct to say "He learns quick" because "quick" is an adjective and cannot modify the verb "learns." The sentence should read, "He learns quickly."

Correct the following sentence.

1. The surgeon operated careful.

_____

FRAME 10

An adjective cannot modify another adjective. Example: He is terrible sick. In the example the adjective "terrible" modifies another adjective, "sick." This is not correct. If you change "terrible" to an adverb, then the sentence is correct: He is terribly sick.

Correct the following sentence.

1. The officer was serious wounded.

_____

FRAME 11

We have previously learned about a predicate adjective construction. Example: The pencil is black. The word "black" is an adjective. A subject complement is another construction. Example: John is a singer. Notice that "John" and "singer" are equal. Now look at a common error: A power failure is when the electricity goes off. The word "when" does not describe "power failure"; therefore the word "when" is not equal or equivalent to "power failure." Correct versions: A power failure occurs when . . . _or_ A power failure is a lack of electricity.

Correct this sentence.

1. Christmas is when the family gets together.

_____

FRAME 12

Let's review this problem. The word following _is_ (or _was, were, be, has been,_ etc.) can be an adjective that describes the subject. It can also be a noun that refers to or means the same as the subject. Thus, you can say "History is useful" or you can say "History is a subject," but you should not say "History is when . . . "

Correct this sentence.

1. Joplin is where he bought the tires.

_____

FRAME 13

In previous frames you learned that adjectives can show degrees of comparison. Examples: old, older, oldest. These degrees of comparison are positive, comparative, and superlative. The positive describes a single thing: It is thin. The comparative compares two things: This paper is thinner than that. The superlative compares three or more things: Pat is the thinnest of the four sisters.

1. To compare two things, use the _____ form.

2. To compare three or more things, use the _____ form.

FRAME 14

Adjectives with more than one syllable (e.g., intelligent) may not sound right with -er or -est added. In such a case, form the comparative by saying *more intelligent;* form the superlative by saying *most intelligent.*

Select the correct comparison in the following sentence.

    1. Betty is (more attractive, attractiver) than her sister.

FRAME 15

The structure of some adverbs changes to show different degrees of intensity or comparison. The adverb *rapidly* is the positive form; *more rapidly* is the comparative form, and *most rapidly* is the superlative form. Adjectives sometimes use -er and -est to form the comparative and the superlative; adverbs do not use those suffixes. The words *more* and *most* generally form the comparative and superlative. Not all adverbs have comparative and superlative forms. Examples: not, when, therefore.

Select the correct comparison in the following sentence.

    1. Officer Jones was able to pursue the suspect (more, most) quickly than his partner.

FRAME 16

Let us review what we have learned. Both adjectives and adverbs are modifiers. Adjectives modify nouns or noun substitutes; they may not modify other adjectives. The articles *a, an,* and *the* are a special group of adjectives. Adverbs modify verbs, adjectives, and other adverbs. Adverbs often end in -ly. Do not use adverbs in constructions such as "A holiday is *when* . . ." or "Hastings is *where* . . ." Adjectives have three degrees of comparison: positive, comparative, and superlative. Some adverbs also have the same three degrees of comparison.

FRAME 17

This frame is a review test of adjectives and adverbs.

Classify the underlined words as adjectives or adverbs.

    1. He said to look <u>carefully</u> at the product. _____

    2. Ken will construct an <u>exact</u> replica. _____

    3. Jerome speaks <u>well</u>. _____

4. Select <u>a green</u> shirt. _____

5. I am <u>totally</u> committed to the program. _____

Underline the correct words in the following sentences.

6. George is (awful, awfully) sick.

7. Monday is (when the, the day that) blues are a problem.

8. Henry is the (taller, tallest) of the pair.

9. Among the six sisters Gretchen is (more, most) careful.

QUIZ

1. Both adjectives and adverbs are _____.

2. An adjective is a word that modifies or describes a(n) _____ or its equivalent.

3. Which of the following are adjectives?
   a. a
   b. an
   c. the
   d. all of the above

4. _____ are adjectives that do not immediately precede the modified noun.

5. Fill in the blank below with the predicate adjective.

   The patrol sergeant's vehicle is blue rather than the traditional black and white. _____

6. An adverb is a word that modifies a(n)_____, a(n) _____, or another _____.

7. Adverbs often end in _____.

8. Adverbs answer the question:
   a. where.
   b. how.
   c. when.
   d. why.
   e. to what degree.
   f. true or false.
   g. all of the above.

9. True   False   An adjective cannot modify another adjective.

10. True   False   A subject complement is a construction like this: Paul is a police officer.

11. True   False   In the above sentence Paul is equal to police officer.

ANSWERS TO FRAMES

Frame 2
1. modifiers

Frame 3
1. the   a   substantial

Frame 4
1. tiresome
2. pale

Frame 5
1. very carefully

Frame 7

Modifier	*Word Modified*
carelessly	worked
several	mistakes

Frame 8
1. adverb: carefully
   verb modified: defused

Frame 9
1. The surgeon operated carefully.

Frame 10
1. The officer was seriously wounded.

Frame 11
1. Christmas is the day when the family gets together.

Frame 12
1. Joplin is the place where he bought the tires.

Frame 13
1. comparative
2. superlative

Frame 14
1. more attractive

Frame 15
1. more

Frame 17
1. adverb
2. adjective
3. adverb
4. adjectives
5. adverb
6. awfully
7. the day that
8. taller
9. most

13

Pronouns

FRAME 1

This segment of programmed learning material will teach some of the important rules regarding the use of pronouns.

Most frames require a response; you will find the correct answer at the end of this chapter. If you miss a question, go back and review the previous frame before going on.

FRAME 2

Pronouns are words that take the place of, or refer back to, nouns or other pronouns. Pronouns enable us to talk about people and things without the constant repetition of a name or word. Notice how awkward this sentence is without the use of pronouns: Mary had to wash Mary's hair before Mary's friend arrived. Notice how the sentence improves with pronouns: Mary had to wash her hair before her friend arrived.

1. Words used in place of nouns are _____.

FRAME 3

Pronouns should refer back to a noun or another pronoun. Example: Gerald picked up the box that his father had given him. The pronoun "him" takes the place of the noun "Gerald." Another example: Anyone can bring his own skates. In the second example the pronoun "his" refers back to the first pronoun "Anyone." The word that a pronoun refers back to is the antecedent of the pronoun. The antecedent of "him" in the first example is "Gerald"; the antecedent of "his" in the second example is "Anyone."

1. The word that a pronoun refers back to is the _____ of a pronoun.

FRAME 4

In the sentences that follow, write the antecedent of the underlined pronoun in the blank at the end of the sentence.

1. Harold is good at running the mile, but <u>he</u> is no good in the sprints. _____

2. Everyone will bring <u>her</u> own plan. _____

3. Henry gave it to <u>me</u>. _____

4. <u>He</u> sat at the end of the pier watching the tide come in.

_____

FRAME 5

The previous exercise showed that it is not always easy to identify the antecedent of a pronoun. Questions 1 and 2 should be easy. However, in question 3 the antecedent of me is the writer or the speaker, whose identity is unknown. In question 4 the pronoun, He, refers back to an antecedent in some other sentence. The antecedent of a pronoun is not always in the same sentence.

True   False   The antecedent of a pronoun will always be in the same sentence as the pronoun.

FRAME 6

The most common pronouns are *I, me, you, he, she, it, we, us, they,* and *them.* Another group of pronouns that shows possession is *my, your, his, her, its, our,* and *their.* Other common pronouns are *who, whom, whose, this, that, these, those, here, there, what, which, every-one, everybody, somebody, nobody, myself, yourself, herself, himself, itself, ourselves,* and *themselves.* Some words that are sometimes used as pronouns include *both, few, some, all, any, none,* and *either.* This list is not complete but contains some of the most common pronouns.

Underline the pronouns in the following sentence.

1. Sam tried to sell me his old car even though I knew it had been in an accident.

FRAME 7

Underline the pronouns in these sentences.

1. He is the person who can solve the problem.

2. It is not blue and it is not green.

3. You can charge gasoline at his station.

4. I am saving this for myself.

FRAME 8

Up to this point we have learned to define and identify pronouns; we have also learned to define antecedents and to identify the antecedents of pronouns. The next topic is the identification of singular and plural pronouns and singular and plural antecedents of pronouns. Some are easy to classify as singular or plural.

Classify these pronouns as singular or plural.

1. I _____

2. him _____

3. them _____

4. you _____

FRAME 9

You may wish to dispute the answer that classifies *you* as plural. *You* can mean one person or more than one; from a grammatical point of view, it is always plural.

Here is a group of words classified as singular: everyone, someone, somebody, nobody, each, every, either, neither.

Identify the pronouns in the following sentence, and classify each as singular or plural.

1. We made the rule about everyone carrying his ID card.

FRAME 10

We have already learned that antecedents may be either nouns or pronouns. Antecedents can be either singular or plural.

Identify the antecedent of the underlined pronoun in each sentence; then classify the antecedent as singular or plural.

1. Bob could hardly carry a tune because <u>he</u> was tone-deaf. _____

2. One of the scouts lost <u>his</u> pack. _____

3. I want to do it by <u>myself</u>. _____

4. Kelly said that <u>it</u> was easy to do. _____

5. The soldiers put up <u>their</u> tents. _____

FRAME 11

Classify the following statements as true or false.

1. True   False   Antecedents of pronouns are always nouns.

2. True   False   Antecedents of pronouns may be pronouns.

3. True   False   Antecedents of pronouns are always pronouns.

4. True   False   Antecedents of pronouns may be either nouns or pronouns.

FRAME 12

Up to this point we have reviewed some basic information about pronouns so that we could apply a basic pronoun rule: A pronoun must agree with its antecedent. Consider this example: The scouts put away their gear. The pronoun "their" refers back to the antecedent "scouts." Both pronoun and antecedent are plural: they agree in number. Here is another example: Joseph opened his pack. The pronoun "his" refers back to the antecedent "Joseph." Both pronoun and antecedent are singular: They agree in number. Complete the following sentence.

1. If a pronoun is plural, then its antecedent must be
_____.

FRAME 13

In the sentences that follow, supply a pronoun that agrees with its antecedent.

1. The employees planned and attended _____ picnic.

2. He was an expert locksmith but seldom practiced _____ trade.

3. We hired an attorney in an attempt to get _____ property back.

FRAME 14

In the last frame we learned that a pronoun must agree with its antecedent in number. It must also agree in gender. Example: Alice waited for her appointment. The pronoun "her" agrees in gender with its antecedent "Alice."

In the sentences that follow, select a pronoun that agrees in gender with its antecedent.

1. The book was lying in the mud with _____ pages open.

2. Henry completed the course; now _____ will go back to work.

3. The actress refused to sign _____ contract.

FRAME 15

Now we come to a situation where it is hard to apply the agreement rule. Note this example: Each officer must bring _____ own weapon. The agreement rule says that the pronoun should be singular, but if we use the pronoun *his,* we indicate that all of the soldiers are men, which may not be true. Since the English language lacks a neuter, the best practice is to use both the masculine and feminine pronouns together separated by a slash (his/her).

Select correct pronouns for the following sentences.

1. Each Camp Fire Girl will bring _____ candy sale record.

2. Every student sang at the top of _____ voice.

3. Someone is waiting for _____ turn.

FRAME 16

Here is some more practice on this problem.

1. Each secretary will bring a sample of _____ work.

2. One vice president lost _____ job.

3. The students rewrote _____ themes.

4. All school board members wrote _____ opinion and passed it in to the chairmen.

FRAME 17

In question 1 there are at least two acceptable pronouns. In question 2 one should use *his* or *her*, depending on the sex of the vice president. In sentence 3 *their* is correct; its antecedent is *students*, which is plural. In sentence 4 the use of the word *their* avoids the gender problem.

FRAME 18

If you remember and apply the rule about making the pronoun agree with its antecedent, then you will avoid most pronoun problems. Another aspect of the agreement rule that deserves special mention is the pronoun that has no known antecedent: It is not possible to determine what the writer is referring to. This sentence is an example: Kelly said that *it* was easy to do. Here you cannot tell what *it* means or refers to unless there is an explanation in another sentence. When you use a pronoun, be sure the reader (or listener) can identify the antecedent of the pronoun.

Select the pronoun that has an indefinite reference to an antecedent.

1. Ken brought along his pack because he wanted to protect it from them. _____

FRAME 19

Another aspect of agreement is that a pronoun, if it is the subject of a sentence, must agree with the verb. You need to remember which of the pronouns are singular and which are plural.

Singular subject pronoun: Someone is here.
Plural subject pronoun: They are here.

Select the verb that agrees with the subject pronoun.

1. Each of the boys (is, are) waiting in line.

2. You (is, are) the best writer.

3. Everyone (was, were) sampling the food.

4. They (work, works) at the mill.

5. Nobody (sings, sing) in tune.

FRAME 20

In summary, here is what you need to remember about pronoun usage. When you use a pronoun, think about its antecedent; make sure there is one and make sure the pronoun agrees with its antecedent. If you use a pronoun as the subject of a sentence, think about whether it is singular or plural; then be sure the verb agrees with its subject. If you have problems making the pronoun agree with its subject, then you may wish to review Chapter 8, Agreement of Subject and Verb.

FRAME 21

This frame is a review test of pronouns.

1. The word a pronoun stands for, or refers back to, is its _____.

Choose the correct pronoun for these sentences.

2. I was afraid I would cut _____ if I used the knife.

3. The employees were sad when they entered the plant for _____ last shift.

4. Our coach was the best _____ could hire.

5. Every soldier held _____ weapon ready for inspection.

Select the correct verb in the following sentence.

6. Everyone (is, are) going to the party.

QUIZ

1. Pronouns are words that take the place of, or refer back to, _____ or other _____.

2. The word that a pronoun refers back to is the _____ of a pronoun.

3. Which of the following pronouns is singular?
   a. everyone
   b. someone
   c. nobody
   d. each
   e. all of the above

4. Which of the following sentences has an antecedent to the underlined pronoun that is plural?
   a. One of the scouts lost <u>his</u> pack.
   b. I want to do it by <u>myself</u>.
   c. Officer Jones misplaced <u>his</u> fingerprint kit.
   d. The soldiers put up <u>their</u> tents.

5. True False Antecedents of pronouns are always nouns.

6. True False Antecedents of pronouns may be either nouns or pronouns.

Choose the correct pronoun for each sentence.

7. The officers submitted _____ reports to the detectives.

8. The officers took us to the location where they recovered _____ property.

9. True False An antecedent must agree in gender with its pronoun.

Choose the correct pronoun.

10. The actress refused to sign _____ contract.

Fill in the blanks.

11. When the gender of the antecedent is unclear (each, someone, everyone, etc.), we use a neuter _____ pronoun, _____.

12. Every student sang at the top of _____ voice.
    a. his
    b. her
    c. their
    d. none of the above

13. A pronoun that is the subject of a sentence must agree in _____ with its verb.

14. Each of the boys _____ waiting in line.
    a. is
    b. are
    c. am

15. None of them _____ able to do the math problem.
    a. is
    b. are
    c. am

ANSWERS TO FRAMES

Frame 2
  1. pronouns

Frame 3
  1. antecedent

Frame 4
  1. Harold
  2. Everyone
  3. the writer or speaker
  4. unknown

Frame 5

1. False

Frame 6

1. me, his, I, it

Frame 7

1. He, who
2. It, it
3. You, his
4. I, this, myself

Frame 8

1. I—singular
2. him—singular
3. them—plural
4. you—plural

Frame 9

1. We—plural
   everyone—singular
   his—singular

Frame 10

1. Bob—singular
2. one—singular
3. I—singular
4. unknown
5. soldiers—plural

Frame 11

1. False
2. True
3. False
4. True

Frame 12

1. plural

Frame 13

1. their
2. his
3. our

Frame 14

1. its
2. he
3. her

Frame 15

1. her
2. his/her
3. his/her

Frame 16

1. his, her, or their
2. his or her
3. their
4. their

Frame 18

1. them

Frame 19

1. is
2. are
3. was
4. work
5. sings

Frame 21

1. antecedent
2. myself
3. their
4. we
5. his or their
6. is

14

Topic Sentences

FRAME 1

This segment of programmed learning material will help you identify and use the topic sentence correctly.

Most frames require a response; you will find the correct answer at the end of this chapter. If you miss a question, go back and review the previous frame before going on.

FRAME 2

The *Random House Dictionary* defines a paragraph as a distinct portion of written or printed matter dealing with a particular idea. This is a good definition; a paragraph deals with a single idea. Paragraphs differ in complexity and length. Newspaper paragraphs tend to be short—perhaps only two or three sentences. In other kinds of written work, paragraphs are longer. Paragraph lengths of more than 50 words and less than 200 words are common.

1. Paragraphs with short sentences are often found in

   _____.

FRAME 3

Most well-written paragraphs contain a topic sentence. A topic sentence states the main idea of a paragraph; it tells the reader what the paragraph will be about. A good paragraph will develop around the central idea stated in the topic sentence.

1. A statement of the central idea developed in the paragraph is the _____.

2. A distinct portion of written or printed matter dealing with a particular idea is a(n) _____.

FRAME 4

Here is an example of a topic sentence used in a paragraph; the underlined portion is the topic sentence:

<u>There are four parts of an ordinary pencil</u>. The main part of a pencil is a wooden cylinder. The wooden cylinder has a hollow core filled with a solid cylinder of graphite. On the top end of the cylinder is a metal ferrule, which attaches a rubber eraser to the pencil.

FRAME 5

The topic sentence in frame 4 told you what the paragraph would be about and how the writer intended to develop the paragraph. The topic sentence implied that the writer would list and explain the parts of a pencil. The topic sentence should tell what the paragraph will be about; it may also tell you how the writer will develop the paragraph.

Read the following sentence and answer the questions that follow.

There were several factors that caused the accident on Fourth Street.

1. True   False   This sentence conforms to the definition of a topic sentence.

2. True   False   The paragraph will describe the accident on Fourth Street.

3. True   False   The paragraph will contain a list of causes of the accident.

FRAME 6

The topic sentence explains what the paragraph will be about. If the paragraph is properly constructed, all the sentences except the topic sentence support the purpose stated in the topic sentence. Making all the sentences in a paragraph support the topic sentence is called paragraph unity.

Topic sentence: Spring flowers appear at different times.
Sentence b: The tulip is among the first of the spring flowers.
Sentence c: Chrysanthemums begin blooming in September.

1. Does sentence b support the topic sentence?

   _____

2. Does sentence c support the topic sentence?

   _____

FRAME 7

In the paragraph that follows, decide which lettered sentences support the purpose stated in the topic sentence. Underlining identifies the topic sentence.

<u>When gasoline began to be scarce and expensive, the major carmakers responded with smaller vehicles that gave better gas mileage</u>. (a) General Motors went through a downsizing process that made most of their models smaller and lighter. (b) Ford produced a smaller model called the Escort. (c) Chrysler produced the smaller front-wheel-drive "K" car.

(d) Not only were cars smaller, but engines also became smaller as four-cylinder engines became popular again. (e) Small size, small engines, front-wheel-drive, and economy became essential elements of the auto industry.

1. Which sentences support the topic sentence? _____

   _____

FRAME 8

From among the three lettered sentences, select one choice that best supports the topic sentence. Underlining identifies the topic sentence.

<u>Various kinds of wood have distinctive qualities that make them useful for specific purposes</u>. (a) Wood is dry when it is cut into boards. (b) Cedar is resistant to rot, so it is useful for fence posts. (c) Walnut trees can be a valuable long-term resource.

1. Which sentence choice best supports the topic sentence?

   _____

FRAME 9

Read the following sentences; then select an appropriate topic sentence from among choices a, b, and c.

Zoysia grass is attractive and resistant to dry, hot weather, but it turns brown early in the autumn and stays brown. Fescue is a tough, durable grass, but it is not especially attractive. Bluegrass is a good choice; it does well in spring and autumn but does not do so well in hot, dry weather.

a. Several varieties of grass are available to the Midwestern homeowner who must try to grow grass in a rather hostile environment.
b. Grasses from the far north do well in the Midwest.
c. Growing a good lawn is not easy.

Which choice makes the best topic sentence? _____

FRAME 10

Up to this point, all the examples have shown the topic sentence as the first sentence in the paragraph. The topic sentence may be in any position in the paragraph but is usually near the beginning of the paragraph. Underlining identifies the topic sentence in the following paragraph:

I started that particular day by oversleeping and missing breakfast. When I drove out of the garage, I found that I had a flat tire. While changing the tire, I got my shirt dirty and had to go back and change my shirt. <u>It was one of those days when everything went wrong</u>.

FRAME 11

From among the lettered sentences in the following paragraph, select the topic sentence.

(a) Some of the older health rules are no longer valid. (b) There is a new set of health rules that can contribute to your feeling of well-being and lengthen your life span. (c) One rule is to refrain from smoking. (d) Another rule is to keep your weight down. (e) Exercise vigorously and regularly. (f) Get an adequate amount of rest. (g) Do not use alcohol excessively. (h) These rules, if followed conscientiously, can improve or maintain a high standard of health.

1. Which lettered sentence makes the best topic sentence?

   _____

FRAME 12

Although sentence h is a summary sentence, it could also serve as a topic sentence.

Here is a summary of the major points covered in this instructional material. A paragraph deals with a particular idea. Most paragraphs have a topic sentence, which explains what the paragraph is about. The topic sentence is often near the beginning of the paragraph but can be anywhere in the paragraph. All sentences in the paragraph should relate to the topic sentence.

FRAME 13

Here are some final words on the topic sentence. Good writers use topic sentences. A topic sentence helps writers to organize their thoughts, and it tells the reader what the paragraph will be about. Your writing will be better if you remember to make use of the topic sentence in your writing.

QUIZ

1. Most well-written paragraphs contain a(n) _____.

2. A(n) _____ states the main idea of a paragraph.

3. From among the three choices below, select one that supports the following topic sentence: Handguns come in various types.
    a. Semi-automatics are best because they hold the most rounds of all.
    b. First, there are revolvers.
    c. A six-inch barrel is more accurate than a four-inch barrel.

4. Topic sentences are normally found near the _____ of a paragraph.

5. Select the topic sentence from among the following:
    a. There were prominent "drag" indentations in the rug.
    b. In the bedroom we found the body of a young woman.
    c. The proper gathering of evidence was crucial to the investigation.
    d. Inside the house, in the living room, there were several 9mm casings.
    e. There was a blood trail into the house.

6. True   False   The topic sentence should tell what the paragraph will be about.

7. True   False   The topic sentence may tell you how the writer will develop the paragraph.

8. If a paragraph is properly constructed, which sentences support the purpose stated in the topic sentence?
    a. some of the sentences
    b. all of the sentences
    c. the second and last sentences
    d. none of the above

ANSWERS TO FRAMES

Frame 2
1. newspapers

Frame 3
1. topic sentence
2. paragraph

Frame 5
1. True
2. False
3. True

Frame 6
1. yes
2. no

Frame 7
1. all (a, b, c, d, and e)

Frame 8
1. b

Frame 9
1. a

Frame 11
1. (b) or (h)

15

Case of Pronouns

FRAME 1

This segment of programmed learning material will teach some of the important rules about the case of pronouns.

You need to learn about the case of pronouns so that you know when to use *I* and when to use *me*. There are other pronouns that cause problems; learning about the case of pronouns will help you to avoid pronoun problems.

Most frames require a response; you will find the correct answer at the end of this chapter. If you miss a question, go back and review the previous frame before going on.

FRAME 2

Case applies mostly to pronouns. There are three different cases of pronouns: nominative (or subjective), objective, and possessive.

The function of the pronoun determines its case: If the function of the pronoun is to be the subject of the sentence, then use the nominative (or subjective) form; if the function of a pronoun is to be an object, then use the objective form; and if the function of the pronoun is to show possession, then use the possessive form.

1. The three cases of pronouns are _____ or

_____, _____, and

_____.

FRAME 3

Case applies more to pronouns than nouns. Notice this pair of examples:

She prepared a meal for him.
He prepared a meal for her.

When we switch the pronoun "him" to the first part of the sentence, its function changes and its form changes. (Read that again and think about it.)

Switch the pronouns "I" and "them" in the following sentence and notice the change in form.

I bought the books for them.

1. _____ bought the books for _____.

FRAME 4

Now let's try the same thing with a pair of nouns:

Harold chased the dogs.
The dogs chased Harold.

Notice that the form of a noun does not change when its position and function change.

FRAME 5

Now let's see how the pronoun *I* changes according to its case: I—nominative, me—objective, my or mine—possessive. The general rules require use of the nominative form when the pronoun is the subject of a sentence and require use of the objective form if the pronoun is the object of a sentence; if the pronoun shows possession, use the possessive form of the pronoun. We will consider each of these rules in detail.

1. If a pronoun is the subject of a sentence, then use a pronoun in the _____ or _____ case.

2. When a pronoun is an object in the sentence, then use a pronoun in the _____ case.

3. If the pronoun shows possession, then use the _____ case.

FRAME 6

Here is a list of personal pronouns in the three cases. You will probably want to refer to this list.

Nominative	*Objective*	*Possessive*
I	me	my, mine
you	you	your, yours
she	her	her, hers
he	him	his
it	it	its
we	us	our, ours
they	them	their, theirs
who	whom	whose
whoever	whomever	whosoever

Only personal pronouns change from one case to another. Other pronouns have a single form.

FRAME 7

If a personal pronoun is the subject of a sentence, then use the nominative form of the pronoun. This causes very few problems. "Us are good" and "Me is happy" are obviously wrong. If there is more than one subject, it is more difficult. The presence of prepositional phrases or other words may make it difficult to identify the subject.

Select the correct pronoun for the following sentences.

1. John and (I, me) were the first in line.

2. Henry and (she, her) argue all the time.

3. In the meantime Bob and (he, him) found the answer.

FRAME 8

Use the nominative or subjective form of the pronoun with a subjective complement. Underlining identifies the subjective complements in these examples:

1. John is the <u>author</u> of the book.
2. It is <u>I</u>.
3. Who is <u>he</u>?

The subjective complement completes the subject, or it is equal to the subject: "John" equals "author"; "It" equals "I"; "Who" equals "he."

Select the correct pronoun for these sentences.

1. That was (he, him) in the green shirt.

2. "Is this Barbara?" "This is (she, her)."

FRAME 9

These answers are not so obvious. In sentence 1 "That" equals "he," and in sentence 2 "This" equals "she." Both "he" and "she" are subject complements that require the nominative case.

Select the correct pronoun for the sentences that follow.

1. It was (he, him) who was in error.

2. It was (I, me) who was already prepared.

FRAME 10

We have taught you to use the nominative form of the pronoun when the pronoun is a subjective complement. Several incorrect usages such as "It's me" and "It's him" are common in everyday speech and in informal writing. Even so, you should know the correct forms and use correct forms in your writing even if you do not use correct forms in your speech.

State the correct pronoun for the incorrect usages in sentences 1 and 2.

1. It's me. _____

2. It's him. _____

FRAME 11

We need to do a brief review of clauses before the next teaching point. A clause is a group of words containing both subject and verb; independent clauses can stand alone as complete sentences, but dependent clauses cannot stand alone. Example: When he came to the fork in the path, John stopped and looked in both directions. The dependent clause is "When he came to the fork in the path." The other clause is an independent clause.

1. A(n) _____ clause contains a subject and verb and can stand alone; a(n) _____ clause contains a subject and verb but cannot stand alone as a sentence.

FRAME 12

If a pronoun is the subject of a clause, either dependent or independent, then use the nominative form of the pronoun (underlined in the example). Example: Since <u>we</u> began the lessons, <u>she</u> is improving greatly.

Select the correct pronoun forms for this sentence.

1. While Peter and (he, him) opened the box, Paul and (I, me) stood and watched.

FRAME 13

Since you use the objective form of a pronoun when the pronoun is a direct object, you need to be able to identify direct objects. A direct object receives the action of a verb. Example: The dog chased Roy and him. In the example both "Roy" and "him" are direct objects; both receive action.

Identify the direct objects in these sentences.

1. Bob, the barber, cut my hair.

2. Henry called Bob and me.

3. He opened the box.

FRAME 14

The rule says that you should use the objective form if the pronoun is the direct object of a sentence. This is more likely to cause trouble when there is more than one direct object.

Select the correct pronoun in the following sentences.

1. The policeman arrested Tom and (he, him).

2. The suspect tied (him, he) and (I, me) to a tree.

FRAME 15

Since you use the objective case of the pronoun when the pronoun is an object of a preposition, there is a need to review the definition and identification of prepositional phrases. A preposition is a word that relates a noun or pronoun to some other word in the sentence. Some common prepositions are *in, on, to, with, by, at,* and *through.* Examples of prepositional phrases: at my house, in the meadow, with Tom, by myself, at the movies.

Identify the prepositional phrases in the following sentence.

1. We walked to the pasture with George and watched the horses.

FRAME 16

The rule requires the use of the objective case of the pronoun when a pronoun is the object of a preposition. Let's analyze a typical prepositional phrase: in the chair. In this phrase "in" is a preposition and "chair" is the object of a preposition; "the" is an adjective that modifies "chair."

Identify the object of the preposition in each of the following prepositional phrases.

1. with the new English teacher

2. with Randolph and me

3. through the passage

4. by me and him

FRAME 17

Note that the answers to questions 2 and 4 both have more than one object of a preposition.

In the sentences that follow, select the correct pronouns.

1. Elmer found Karen and (I, me) at the club.

2. She gave the award to Captain Clark and (I, me).

3. She and (I, me) performed for (he, him) and Kate.

4. For George and (I, me), it was a waste of time.

FRAME 18

The first choice in sentence 3 is "I" because both "She" and "I" are subjects; "him" and "Kate" are both objects of the preposition "for." In sentence 4 the prepositional phrase begins the sentence; "me" is correct because it is the object of the preposition "for."

Let's review. Use the nominative form of the pronoun when the pronoun is a subject or part of a subject; you also use it when a pronoun is a subjective complement. Use the objective form of the pronoun with personal pronouns used as direct objects or as objects of prepositions.

FRAME 19

Use the objective form of a personal pronoun when a pronoun is an indirect object. An indirect object indicates to whom or for whom something was done. The indirect object occurs with verbs of asking, giving, telling, receiving, etc. In a sentence it always comes before the direct object. Example: Henry paid me the money. The word "me" is the indirect object; it comes before the direct object "money."

Select the indirect objects in the following sentences.

1. Father bought her a new motorcycle.

2. My brother gave Bob a gift.

FRAME 20

A further explanation of the indirect object is that it is like a prepositional phrase with the preposition omitted. Example: He gave the baby some candy. A test to determine its usage as an indirect object is to insert the preposition *to* and see if it would fit into the sentence. It is very awkward to insert the word *to* before "some" or "candy," but you can insert it before "the baby": He gave (to) the baby some candy.

Select the indirect objects in these sentences.

1. The boss gave Bob and me a bonus.

2. The coach gave us a lecture.

FRAME 21

Use the objective form of a pronoun when a pronoun is a direct object, an indirect object, or an object of a preposition. Remember that the rule applies even when there are two or more pronouns.

In the sentences that follow, underlining identifies certain pronouns; identify the usage of each pronoun.

1. He brought flowers for <u>her</u>. _____

2. The barber shaved <u>him</u>. _____

3. Kelly provided <u>her</u> and <u>him</u> an alibi. _____

4. The teacher chose <u>him</u> for lunchroom duty. _____

FRAME 22

In the sentences that follow, select the correct pronouns.

1. The sergeant chose Roger and (I, me) for the job.

2. For Mary and (I, me), the task was boring.

3. We gave Betty and (they, them) farewell gifts.

4. Colonel Craft provided an example for my brother and (I, me).

FRAME 23

Before going on to the next point, let's consider the pronouns *who* and *whom*. These pronouns often cause problems. *Who* is the nominative form, and *whom* is the objective form. It is correct to say "Who is at the door?" because "Who" is the subject. It is correct to say "To whom do you wish to speak?" because "whom" is the object of the preposition "To."

Select the correct pronoun in the following sentences.

1. (Who, Whom) is the fairest of them all?

2. For (who, whom) are you looking?

FRAME 24

Who and *whom* cause problems because of their use in constructions where word order is unusual. Example: Whom did you give the order to? The verb is "give" or "did give"; the subject of the verb is "you," and "Whom" is the object of the preposition "to" at the end of the sentence. The example can be recast to read: You did give the order to whom? That sounds awkward but shows why "Whom" is correct.

Select the correct pronoun in these sentences.

1. (Who, Whom) called after midnight?

2. (Who, Whom) did you see in the city?

FRAME 25

Another special problem occurs with the use of pronouns as appositives. An appositive is a word or phrase that is placed next to a noun or pronoun and that identifies or explains it by renaming it. Example: We teachers always stick together. Note that "We" equals "teachers"; note that "We teachers" is a subject, so the use of *we* rather than *us* is correct. Another example: He will send the data to us teachers. Here "us" equals "teachers"; note that "us teachers" is the object of the preposition "to," so the use of *us* rather than *we* is correct.

Select the correct pronoun for these sentences.

1. It is important for (us, we) the living to remember the sacrifices of others.

2. For (we, us) soldiers, early rising is easy.

FRAME 26

Another special problem regarding case concerns constructions such as "George is smarter than (he, him)." To analyze this sentence, think of the sentence as saying that "George is smarter than he (is smart)." The last part of the sentence, "(is smart)," is understood; it is easy to see why "he" is the correct pronoun.

Analyze and select the correct pronouns for these sentences.

1. Pinky runs faster than (I, me).

2. Judy is older than (she, her).

3. Their group is more clumsy than (we, us).

4. Captain Green is taller than (her, she).

FRAME 27

The remaining case for consideration is the possessive case; the possessive case shows possession. The possessive form is often a subject complement. Examples: That crop is ours. That book is mine. Is this umbrella hers? Note the use of a slightly different form when the pronoun is immediately before the noun: It is *our* crop, *my* book, and *her* umbrella.

Select the correct pronoun in the following sentences.

1. This is (your, yours).

2. Wallace returned (their, theirs) book.

3. This will be (my, mine) last year.

FRAME 28

Let's review the general ideas about case. The function of a pronoun determines its case. If it functions as a subject, a subjective complement, or an appositive of a subject, then you use the nominative form. If the pronoun functions as a direct object, an indirect object, or an object of a preposition, then you use the objective form. If the function is to show possession, then use the possessive form.

FRAME 29

In the sentences that follow, numbers and underlining identify certain words. State the function of the numbered, underlined word. For example, the function of (1) is subject; (3) shows possession.

1. <u>You</u> can give   2. <u>Brenda</u>   3. <u>her</u>
4. <u>lesson</u> now   5. <u>She</u> played   6. <u>one</u> of the songs in
7. <u>her</u> second book while   8. <u>she</u> and   9. <u>I</u> waited for
10. <u>you</u>.

1. _____   2. _____

3. _____   4. _____

5. _____   6. _____

7. _____   8. _____

9. _____   10. _____

FRAME 30

Frame 31 is a review test. You should determine the function of the pronoun so that you can determine the proper case of the pronoun.

FRAME 31

This frame is a review test of pronouns.

1. It is (she, her) in the picture.

2. We gave Bob and (he, him) a party.

3. For the better part of an hour, Dave and (I, me) fought the giant fish.

4. For Tracy and (I, me), skiing was easy.

5. While (we, us) pedestrians waited, the convoy passed by.

6. (Who, Whom) are you talking to?

7. Kay drove Jerry and (I, me) to the club.

8. The bags are (their, theirs).

9. While (he, him) and George waited, we repaired the damage.

10. Tony can run faster than (I, me).

QUIZ

1. There are three cases of pronouns. They are _____
   or _____, _____, and
   _____.

2. If a pronoun is the subject of a sentence, then use a pronoun
   in the _____ or _____ case.

3. When a pronoun is an object of a sentence, then use a pronoun in the _____ case.

4. If the pronoun shows possession, then use the
   _____ case.

5. In the meantime, Bob and _____ found the answer.
   a. he
   b. him
   c. neither of the above

6. Use the _____ or _____ form of
   the pronoun with a subjective complement.

7. It is _____.
   a. I
   b. me
   c. neither of the above

8. We use the objective form of a pronoun if the pronoun is the
   _____ _____ of a sentence or
   the object of a(n) _____ _____.

9. Select the correct pronoun in the following sentence.

   Elmer found Karen and _____ at the club.
   a. I
   b. me
   c. neither of the above

10. A(n) _____ _____ indicates to
    whom or for whom something was done.

11. The _____ _____ always comes
    before the direct object.

12. Use the objective form of a pronoun when a pronoun is a(n):
    a. direct object.
    b. indirect object.
    c. object of preposition.
    d. all of the above.

ANSWERS TO FRAMES

Frame 2

  1. nominative or subjective, objective, and possessive (any order)

Frame 3

  1. They   me

Frame 5

  1. nominative or subjective
  2. objective
  3. possessive

Frame 7

  1. I
  2. She
  3. he

Frame 8

  1. he
  2. she

Frame 9

  1. he
  2. I

Frame 10

  1. I
  2. he

Frame 11

  1. independent   dependent

Frame 12

  1. he   I

Frame 13

  1. hair
  2. Bob, me
  3. box

Frame 14

  1. him
  2. him, me

Frame 15

  1. to the pasture   with George

Frame 16

  1. teacher (or English teacher)
  2. Randolph, me
  3. passage
  4. me, him

Frame 17

  1. me
  2. me
  3. I, him
  4. me

Frame 19

  1. her
  2. Bob

Frame 20

  1. Bob, me
  2. us

Frame 21

  1. her—object of preposition
  2. him—direct object
  3. her, him—indirect objects
  4. him—direct object

Frame 22

  1. me
  2. me
  3. them
  4. me

Frame 23

  1. Who
  2. whom

Frame 24

  1. Who
  2. Whom

Frame 25

  1. us
  2. us

Frame 26

1. I
2. she
3. we
4. she

Frame 27

1. yours
2. their
3. my

Frame 29

1. subject
2. indirect object
3. shows possession
4. direct object
5. subject

6. direct object
7. shows possession
8. subject
9. subject
10. object of preposition

Frame 31

1. she
2. him
3. I
4. me
5. we
6. Whom
7. me
8. theirs
9. he
10. I

16

Spelling

FRAME 1

This segment of programmed learning material will help you to improve your spelling by teaching some basic spelling rules and by providing you with some useful advice.

Most frames require a response; you will find the correct answer at the end of the chapter. If you miss a question, go back and review the previous frame before going on.

FRAME 2

Going through this programmed learning material will not suddenly transform you into an expert speller. If you read and work through this material slowly and carefully and if you accept the advice provided, you will improve your spelling.

In some languages, such as Polish and Spanish, the pronunciation of a word indicates the spelling of that word; sometimes this is true in English, but often it is not true.

FRAME 3

We will begin with spelling rules. Perhaps the most common spelling rule is the one that says

Write *i* before *e*
Except after *c*
Or when it sounds like *a*
As in neighbor and weigh.

Use the rule to select the correct spelling of the following.

1. theif or thief _____

2. vein or vien _____

3. ceiling or cieling _____

FRAME 4

Prefixes and suffixes can cause spelling problems. One such problem is what to do with a final *e* when adding a suffix to the word. Consider the word *write* and the suffix *-ing*. The rule is this: When a word ends in *e* and the suffix begins with a vowel, then drop the final *e*. Therefore, *write* plus *-ing* will be *writing*. Other examples: ride + ing = riding; guide + ance = guidance; quote + ation = quotation.

Use the rule to combine the following words and suffixes.

1. use + ing _____

2. promote + able _____

3. inspire + ing _____

FRAME 5

In the last frame we learned this: On words ending in *e*, you drop the final *e* when the suffix begins with a vowel. Suppose that the suffix begins with a consonant. In that case the rule is this: On words ending in *e*, you retain the *e* when the suffix begins with a consonant. Here are two examples: arrange + ment = arrangement; like + ness = likeness.

Use the rules to add suffixes to the following words.

1. sure + ly _____

2. locate + ion _____

3. manage + ment _____

FRAME 6

Now we will learn a rule that concerns words ending in *y*. The rule is this: Change the final *y* to an *i* when adding a suffix unless the suffix begins with *i*. Here are two examples: defy + *ance* = defiance; modify + *er* = modifier.

Use the rule in adding suffixes to the following.

    1. qualify + er _____

    2. forty + eth _____

    3. dry + ing _____

FRAME 7

The next spelling rule concerns one-syllable words that end in a consonant preceded by a vowel. To add a suffix, you should double the final consonant. Examples: nod, nodding; run, runner; dig, digger.

    The previous paragraph gave a rule for suffixes beginning with a vowel. If the suffix does not begin with a vowel, you do *not* double the final consonant. Examples: ship, shipment; gun, gunboat; wig, wigless.

Apply the rules to these words and suffixes.

    1. star + ship _____

    2. star + ing _____

    3. bed + bug _____

    4. sad + en _____

    5. bed + ing _____

    6. red + leg _____

FRAME 8

Most words form their plurals by adding -*s*; however, if adding the letter *s* creates an extra syllable, then add -*es* to make the plural. Example: When you make the word *bush* plural, you pronounce it as two syllables; the same is true of *bunch, tax,* and *pass.* Adding -*s* to *boy, waffle,* or *tile* will not create an extra syllable.

Write the plurals of these words.

    1. crutch _____

    2. sex _____

    3. church _____

    4. handle _____

FRAME 9

Another rule applies to nouns ending in *y* preceded by a consonant: These nouns form their plural by changing the *y* to *i* and adding *-es*. Examples: body, bodies; candy, candies.

Use the rule to change the following words to their plural form.

1. ferry _____

2. shanty _____

3. mercy _____

FRAME 10

This rule concerns words ending in *y* and preceded by a single vowel. Such words require only the addition of the letter *s*. Examples: key, keys; boy, boys; toy, toys.

Use the rules for words ending in *y* to form plurals of the following.

1. day _____

2. family _____

3. fly _____

4. quantity _____

5. clay _____

FRAME 11

This is a review test to see if you can apply the spelling rules.

Underline the correct spelling for each item.

1. receive or recieve

2. tireing or tiring

3. rarely or rarly

4. qualities or qualitys

5. claped or clapped

6. speechs or speeches

7. belfries or befrys

8. toys, toies, or toyes

FRAME 12

A final word about spelling rules: There are some exceptions to the rules, but learning and using rules will make you a better speller.

FRAME 13

The next topic is homophones. Homophones are pairs of words pronounced the same, or nearly the same, but having different meanings; they may also have different spellings. To spell a word correctly, you must know which word you are spelling. We will begin with this troublesome group.

> their—possessive form of they
> they're—contraction of they are
> there—means in that place

Write the correct form of each homophone in the following sentences.

1. Ask them if _____ going to the party.

2. Please put it over _____.

3. All the skaters lost _____ hats.

FRAME 14

Another group of problem homophones is to, too, two. Here is a list of meanings.

> two—the number; sum of one and one
> too—in addition; also; an excessive amount
> to—a preposition meaning in that direction

Write the correct form of each homophone in the following sentences.

1. The coach has already gone _____ London.

2. Marion added _____ much salt.

3. One-half of four is _____.

4. James is _____ tall for his clothes.

FRAME 15

The homophones your and you're sometime create problems. Remember that your is a possessive pronoun used in constructions such as this: your hat. The other word, you're, is a contraction of two words: you are.

Write the correct form of each homophone in the following sentences.

1. I can't understand why _____ so uncomfortable.

2. He has found _____ passport.

FRAME 16

Here are two homophones that often cause spelling problems.

allot—to divide or apportion
a lot—two words: the article *a* and the word *lot;* means often or a large amount
Alot—no such word; an incorrect spelling of a lot

Write the correct form of each homophone in the following sentences.

1. Our search uncovered _____ of old bottles.

2. I plan to _____ the portions among the three children.

FRAME 17

Another problem pair is its and it's.

its—a possessive pronoun; does not have or need an apostrophe.
it's—a contraction for it is.

Write the correct form of each homophone in the following sentences.

1. The cat chased _____ tail in a circle.

2. _____ as easy as taking candy from a baby.

FRAME 18

The words loose and lose are not true homophones because their pronunciations are not identical. Nevertheless, they create confusion.

loose—free from restraint
lose—a verb that means you no longer hold or possess something

Write the correct word in the following sentences.

1. When we got home, we found that the dogs were _____.

2. I did not play because I didn't want to _____ more money.

3. Don't _____ your way on the trail.

FRAME 19

There are several things you can do about spelling problems. One action you can take is a careful proofreading of your written work. Get another police officer or correctional officer to look at your work if possible; otherwise, do it yourself. Computer spell checking programs are helpful, but you may not have access to a computer. Moreover, if the word you have misspelled is truly a word, the computer will not recognize it as misspelled. Another thing you can do is to think up a gimmick to help you remember the spelling of a word. Suppose you need to remember that the correct spelling is independent, not independant. Try this: There are no ants in independent. Or: An ant is not independent.

FRAME 20

When you need to remember that there are two c's in accident, you remember that two cars (two c's) create an accident.

It is a good idea to keep a list of words you find difficult to spell. The following are the words that are most frequently misspelled by law enforcement and correctional officers: *affiant, affidavit, chief, lieutenant, misdemeanor, subpoena,* and *warrant.* You can practice spelling the words on your list and those above until you master these problem words.

QUIZ

1. Write _____ before _____, except after _____ or when it sounds like _____, as in _____ and _____.

2. When a word ends in _____ and the suffix begins with a _____, drop the final _____.

3. On words ending in _____, you retain the _____ when the suffix begins with a consonant.

4. Change the final _____ to an *i* when adding a suffix unless the suffix begins with *i.*

5. With one-syllable words that end in a consonant preceded by a _____, when adding a _____ double the final consonant.

6. True or False   Referring to question number 5, if the suffix *does not* begin with a vowel, you *do not* double the final consonant.

7. Most words form their plurals by adding _____; however, if adding the letter _____ creates an extra syllable, then add _____ to make the plural.

8. Homophones are:
   a. two words with the same meaning.
   b. words with several meanings.
   c. pairs of words pronounced the same, or nearly the same, but having different meanings; they may also be spelled differently.
   d. none of the above.

ANSWERS TO FRAMES

Frame 3
1. thief
2. vein
3. ceiling

Frame 4
1. using
2. promotable
3. inspiring

Frame 5
1. surely
2. location
3. management

Frame 6
1. qualifier
2. fortieth
3. drying

Frame 7
1. starship
2. starring
3. bedbug

4. sadden
5. bedding
6. redleg

Frame 8
1. crutches
2. sexes
3. churches
4. handles

Frame 9
1. ferries
2. shanties
3. mercies

Frame 10
1. days
2. families
3. flies
4. quantities
5. clays

Frame 11
1. receive
2. tiring

3. rarely
4. qualities
5. clapped
6. speeches
7. belfries
8. toys

Frame 13

1. they're
2. there
3. their

Frame 14

1. to
2. too
3. two
4. too

Frame 15

1. you're
2. your

Frame 16

1. a lot
2. allot

Frame 17

1. its
2. it's

Frame 18

1. loose
2. lose
3. lose

Answers to End-of-Chapter Quizzes

CHAPTER ONE   INTRODUCTION

1. The six basic qualities of a good report are:

   accurate   clear
   complete   concise
   factual   objective

2. True   <u>False</u>   Field notes are not subject to subpoena.

2. <u>True</u>   False   It is best to separate notes with a title page.

4. The best note-taking method is to take your notes <u>chronologically</u>.

5. True   <u>False</u>   Note-taking is less important for security officers.

CHAPTER TWO   WRITING IN THE ACTIVE VOICE

1. When the subject of the sentence acts, or performs, the verb is in the <u>active voice</u>.

2. When the subject of the sentence receives action, the verb is in the <u>passive voice</u>.

Classify the following sentences as to whether the subject performs or receives the action.

3. Officer Jones was called to the scene by his sergeant. <u>receives action</u>

4. Officer Williams chased the suspect. <u>performs action</u>

5. The fleeing suspect was pursued by Officer O'Reilly who drove dangerously fast. __receives action__

6. The poorly written report was returned to Officer Holden by his sergeant, Joe Friday. __receives action__

7. There are two ways to identify passive voice. The first way is to ask yourself, "Is the subject of the sentence __performing__ or __receiving__ the action of the verb?"

8. The second way to identify passive voice is to determine if the verb is in two parts: one part is a form of the verb **to be**, and the other part is a __past participle__ form of another verb.

9. The different forms of the verb *to be* are: <u>am, are, is, was, were, be, being,</u> and <u>been</u>.

10. Which of the following is in the past participle form?
    a. believe
    b. know
    c. work
    d. discovered

11. Which of the following is in the past participle form?
    a. pursue
    b. arrest
    c. begun
    d. interrogate

12. Which of the following is a combination of a *to be* verb plus a part participle form of another verb?
    a. was seen
    b. will do
    c. has made
    d. none of the above

Using the rules you have been taught, classify the following sentences as active or passive.

13. The trace evidence was carefully packaged by the evidence technician. __passive voice__ .

14. The pit bull was seriously injured by a round from Officer Zimmerman's handgun. __passive voice__

15. Officer Wong has always preferred patrol over investigation. __active voice__

16. Sergeant Good is being divorced by his wife of ten years. __passive voice__

17. The grammatical term __voice__ deals with whether the subject of a sentence acts or receives action.

18. The words *am, are, was,* and *is* are all different forms of the verb <u>to be</u>.

19. Which of the following verbs is in the past participle form? ring, rang, rung <u>rung</u>

20. Which of the following verbs is in the past participle form of the verb? blown, blow, blew <u>blown</u>

21. There are three reasons why we must use the *active voice* in writing reports. Which of the following is *not* a reason?
    a. The active voice tells the reader who is doing the action.
    b. The active voice is efficient.
    c. The active voice is direct, natural, forceful, and easy to understand.
    d. The active voice allows the subject to receive the action rather than perform it.

22. "The handgun was found in the bushes." This is a passive voice sentence that defies which rule(s) above in question 21? (Answer with the multiple-choice letter.) <u>a, b, c</u>

23. "The suspect was pursued by the police dog for ten blocks." This is a passive voice sentence that defies which rule(s) above? (Give letter[s].) <u>b, c</u>

24. "The penal code should be consulted before it is decided which section to use in your report." This is a passive voice sentence that defies which rule(s) above? (Give letter[s].) <u>a, b, c</u>

CHAPTER SEVEN   VERB FORMS AND TENSES

1. In English, verbs have three main forms or principal parts. These three forms are __present__, __past__, and __past participle__.

2. Regular verbs are verbs that add -ed to make the __past__ and __past participle__ forms.

3. Verbs are irregular when their __past__ and __past participle__ forms <u>do not</u> end with __-ed__.

4. Past participle means that the action of the sentence happened
    a. yesterday.
    b. two days ago.
    c. over a period of time in the past.
    d. none of the above.

5. There are three simple tenses. They are __present__ , __past__ , and __future__ .

6. All of the perfect tenses use the __past participle__ form of the verb.

7. All of the perfect tenses require one or more __helping__ verbs.

8. __True__ False   Shifts in tense should be avoided.

9. To form the present perfect tense, you use the helping verb __has__ or __have__ and the __past participle__ .

10. To form the future perfect tense, you use the two helping verbs __will__ and have (*or* __shall__ and __have__), and the __past participle__ .

11. The -*ing* form is the __present participle__ .

CHAPTER EIGHT   AGREEMENT OF SUBJECT AND VERB

1. Every English sentence contains a(n) __subject__ and __verb__ .

2. The subject of the sentence is usually in the __first part__ of the sentence.

3. To make the subject agree with the verb, you must first __identify__ the subject.

4. Which of the following is a prepositional phrase?
   a. in the morning
   b. by myself
   c. at the end
   d. all of the above

5. __True__ False   A prepositional phrase seldom functions as the subject.

6. __True__ False   There can be more than one subject of a sentence.

7. Subjects are plural if the form of the subject indicates more than __one__ .

8. Which of the following is an example of a plural subject.
   a. I
   b. child
   c. we
   d. king

9. The subject is plural if two or more subjects are joined by the word __and__ .

10. A subject is singular if there are two or more subjects joined by the word __or__ or __nor__ .

11. A verb expresses __action__ or __state of being__ .

12. Which of the following is a verb phrase?
    a. was
    b. asked
    c. saw
    d. shall have been

13. The rule on agreement of subject and verb __does__ __not__ __apply__ if the subject is *I, we,* or *you.*

14. The rule on agreement of subject and verb applies only in the __present tense__ .

15. The agreement rule is this: A singular subject requires a(n) __singular verb__ ; a plural subject requires a(n) __plural verb__ .

16. In general, the singular form of verbs ends in a(n) __s__ .

17. In general, the plural form of verbs does __not__ end in a(n) __s__ .

CHAPTER NINE   CAPITALIZATION

1. There is one overall general rule that covers most spelling situations. This is to capitalize:
    a. specific things.
    b. common things.
    c. general things.
    d. none of the above.

2. Always capitalize the pronoun __I__ .

3. Always capitalize the __first__ word of a sentence.

4. Which of the following is correct?
    a. c.i.a.
    b. n.b.c.
    c. c.b.s.
    d. ABC

5. Which of the following is correct?
    a. City
    b. River
    c. California
    d. County

6. Which of the following is correct?
   a. tuesday
   b. March
   c. fourth of july
   d. christmas day

7. Which of the following is correct?
   a. *huckleberry finn*
   b. *a street car named desire*
   c. *Los Angeles Times*
   d. "twinkle, twinkle little star"

8. Capitalize titles when used with the name of a(n) __specific person__.

9. Capitalize a relationship word when used with a(n) __specific name__.

10. Which of the following is correct?
    a. Officer Smith drove southbound on Church Street.
    b. The East played the West in the Shrine Game.
    c. The North and the South opposed each other in the Civil War.
    d. All of the above are correct

11. Which of the following is correct?
    a. Summer is my favorite season.
    b. In the winter I go skiing
    c. I love April because it is the beginning of spring
    d. All of the above are correct

12. Which of the following is correct?
    a. I think Anthropology is a fascinating subject.
    b. I took Philosophy 101 last semester.
    c. I would like to learn spanish.
    d. I have learned to appreciate english much better.

CHAPTER TEN PUNCTUATION

1. A set of three periods used to show an omission in quoted material is called a(n) __ellipsis__.

2. Use the hyphen after the prefixes __ex-__, __anti-__, __self-__, and <u>all</u> and before the suffix __-elect__.

3. Use a(n) __hyphen__ to join two or more words that serve as a single adjective before a noun.

4. Which of the following is a correct use of a hyphen?
   a. He is an ex-police officer
   b. Brigadier-General Jackson was known as "Stonewall."
   c. Sulfuric-acid is hazardous
   d. Lieutenant-Governor Davis is running for governor.

5. Use the hyphen to form __compound__ words

6. Which of the following is correct?
   a. secretary-treasurer
   b. father-in-law
   c. do-it-yourselfer
   d. pie-in-the-sky attitude
   e. all of the above

7. __True__   False   The dash (—) is used to show an interruption or abrupt change of thought in the middle of a sentence.

8. The most common use of quotation marks is:
   a. to set off titles of poems, songs, articles, and short stories.
   b. to enclose a direct quotation from either a written or a spoken source.
   c. Neither is more common than the other.

9. Italics or underlining should be used with:
   a. books.
   b. newspapers.
   c. magazines.
   d. all of the above.

10. Other applications of italics are the names of __ships__ and __aircraft__, __titles__ __of__ __works of art__, movies, __television programs__, radio programs, and __record albums__.

11. Which of the following is the proper use of italics or underlining?
    a. The professor talked about ex post facto laws.
    b. John asked me to help him get elected, and there would be a _quid pro quo_.
    c. Whistler's Mother is a famous work of art.
    d. Yellow Submarine is a famous Beatles' album.

CHAPTER ELEVEN   INTERNAL PUNCTUATION

1. A clause contains a(n) __subject__ and a(n) __verb__.

2. A clause is classified as either __main__ or __subordinate__; these clauses are also known as __independent__ and __dependent__ clauses.

3. A(n) <u>independent clause</u> can stand alone as a sentence.

4. A(n) <u>dependent clause</u> cannot stand alone as a sentence.

5. Which of the following can begin a dependent clause?
   a. if
   b. when
   c. while
   d. as
   e. although
   f. all of the above

6. True <u>False</u> There can be only one independent and one dependent clause in any sentence.

7. True <u>False</u> A phrase is a group of related words that has both a subject and verb.

8. The punctuation most often used with phrases is a:
   a. comma.
   b. period.
   c. semicolon.
   d. colon.

9. <u>True</u> False In most sentences the writer should not punctuate prepositional phrases.

10. True <u>False</u> Two independent clauses should be connected with a comma.

11. Connecting two independent clauses with a comma is an error called a(n) <u>comma splice</u>.

12. Two independent clauses can be connected by which of the following punctuation?
    a. and
    b. semicolon
    c. conjunctive adverb
    d. all of the above

13. Which of the following are conjunctive adverbs?
    a. however
    b. indeed
    c. consequently
    d. moreover
    e. all of the above

14. If a dependent clause begins a sentence, a(n) <u>comma</u> sets it off from the rest of the sentence.

15. A word or group of words that provides useful, but not critical, information is a(n) __parenthetical__ element.

16. <u>True</u>   False   Nonrestrictive elements are set off with commas.

17. A parenthetical expression is a group of words that __interrupts the <u>sentence</u>__ but changes the meaning barely at all.

CHAPTER TWELVE   ADJECTIVES AND ADVERBS

1. Both adjectives and adverbs are __modifiers__

2. An adjective is a word that modifies or describes a(n) __noun__ or its equivalent.

3. Which of the following are adjectives?
   a. a
   b. an
   c. the
   d. all of the above

4. __Predicate adjectives__ are adjectives that do not immediately precede the modified noun.

5. Fill in the blank below with the predicate adjective.

   The patrol sergeant's vehicle is blue rather than black and white. __blue__

6. An adverb is a word that modifies a(n) __verb__, a(n) __adjective__, or another __adverb__.

7. Adverbs often end in __-ly__.

8. Adverbs answer the question:
   a. where.
   b. how.
   c. when.
   d. why.
   e. to what degree.
   f. true or false.
   g. all of the above.

9. <u>True</u>   False   An adjective cannot modify another adjective.

10. <u>True</u>   False   A subject complement is a construction like this: Paul is a police officer.

11. <u>True</u>   False   In the above sentence Paul is equal to police officer.

CHAPTER THIRTEEN   PRONOUNS

1. Pronouns are words that take the place of, or refer back to, __nouns__ or other __pronouns__ .

2. The word that a pronoun refers back to is the __antecedent__ of a pronoun.

3. Which of the following pronouns is singular?
    a. everyone
    b. someone
    c. nobody
    d. each
    e. all of the above

4. Which of the following sentences has an antecedent to the underlined pronoun that is plural?
    a. One of the scouts lost his pack.
    b. I want to do it by myself.
    c. Officer Jones misplaced his fingerprint kit.
    d. The soldiers put up their tents.

5. True __False__ Antecedents of pronouns are always nouns.

6. __True__ False Antecedents of pronouns may be either nouns or pronouns.

Choose the correct pronoun for each sentence.

7. The officers submitted _____ reports to the detectives.

8. The officers took us to the location where they recovered _____ property.

9. __True__ False An antecedent must agree in gender with its pronoun.

Choose the correct pronoun.

10. The actress refused to sign __her__ contract.

Fill in the blanks.

11. When the gender of the antecedent is unclear (each, someone, everyone, etc.), we use a neuter __plural__ pronoun, __their__ .

12. Every student sang at the top of _____ voice.
    a. his
    b. her
    c. their
    d. none of the above

13. A pronoun that is the subject of a sentence must agree in __number__ with its verb.

14. Each of the boys _____ waiting in line.
    a. is
    b. are
    c. am

15. None of them _____ able to do the math problem.
    a. is
    b. are
    c. am

CHAPTER FOURTEEN   TOPIC SENTENCES

1. Most well-written paragraphs contain a(n) __topic sentence__ .

2. A(n) __topic sentence__ states the main idea of a paragraph.

3. From among the three choices below, select *one* that supports the following topic sentence: Handguns come in various types.
   a. Semi-automatics are best because they hold the most rounds of all.
   b. First, there are revolvers.
   c. A six-inch barrel is more accurate than a four-inch barrel.

4. Topic sentences are normally found near the __beginning__ of a sentence.

5. Select the topic sentence from among the following:
   a. There were prominent "drag" indentations in the rug.
   b. In the bedroom we found the body of a young woman.
   c. The proper gathering of evidence was crucial to the investigation.
   d. Inside the house, in the living room, there were several 9mm casings
   e. There was a blood trail into the house.

6. __True__ False   The topic sentence should tell what the paragraph will be about.

7. __True__ False   The topic sentence may tell you how the writer will develop the paragraph.

8. If a paragraph is properly constructed, which sentences support the purpose stated in the topic sentence?
   a. some of the sentences
   b. all of the sentences

      c. the second and last sentences

      d. none of the above

CHAPTER FIFTEEN CASE OF PRONOUNS

1. There are three cases of pronouns. They are __subjective__ or __nominative__ , __objective__ , and __possessive__ .

2. If a pronoun is the subject of a sentence, then use a pronoun in the __nominative__ or __subjective__ case.

3. When a pronoun is an object of a sentence, then use a pronoun in the __objective__ case.

4. If the pronoun shows possession, then use the __possessive__ case.

5. In the meantime, Bob and _____ found the answer.
   a. he
   b. him
   c. neither of the above

6. Use the __nominative__ or __subjective__ form of the pronoun with a subject complement.

7. It is _____
   a. I
   b. me
   c. neither of the above

8. We use the objective form of a pronoun if the pronoun is the __direct object__ of a sentence or the object of a(n) __prepositional phrase__ .

9. Select the correct pronouns in the following sentence. Elmer found Karen and _____ at the club.
   a. I
   b. me
   c. neither of the above

10. A(n) __indirect object__ indicates to whom or for whom something was done.

11. The __indirect object__ always comes before the direct object.

12. Use the objective form of a pronoun when a pronoun is a(n):
    a. direct object.
    b. indirect object.

      c. object of preposition.
      d. all of the above.

CHAPTER SIXTEEN   SPELLING

1. Write __i__ before __e__ , except after __c__ or when sounded like __a__ , as in __neighbor__ and __weigh__ .

2. When a word ends in __e__ and the suffix begins with a __vowel__ , drop the final __e__ .

3. On words ending in __e__ , you retain the __e__ when the suffix begins with a consonant.

4. Change the final __y__ to an *i* when adding a suffix unless the suffix begins with *i.*

5. With one-syllable words that end in a consonant preceded by a __vowel__ , when adding a __suffix__ , double the final consonant.

6. __True__   False   Referring to question number 5, if the suffix *does not* begin with a vowel, you *do not* double the final consonant.

7. Most words form their plurals by adding __-s__ ; however, if adding the letter __s__ creates an extra syllable, then add __-es__ to make the plural.

8. Homophones are:
    a. two words with same meaning.
    b. word with several meanings.
    c. pairs of words pronounced the same, or nearly the same, but having different meanings; they may also be spelled differently.
    d. none of the above.

Sample Police and Correctional Report Forms

GENERIC CRIME REPORT
ANYWHERE, CA, POLICE DEPARTMENT

Page __1__ *of* _____ *Pages*   Beat   Incident number   No. of persons arrested   Case number

PERSON 1:   ☐ Complainant   ☐ Business

Last name	First	Middle initial	Sex	Race	DOB

Home address	City, State	Zip	Home phone	Work phone

Business Address/School	City, State	Zip	Occupation	Work hours

PERSON 2:   ☐ Complainant   ☐ Business   ☐ Reporting person   ☐ Witness   ☐ Additional comp. listed on pg. ___

Last name	First	Middle initial	Sex	Race	DOB

Home address	City, State	Zip	Home phone	Work phone

Business address/School	City, State	Zip	Occupation	Work hours

CRIME: ☐ Race, ethnic, religious, sexual orientation involved

Common name	Section/Subsection	Code	Date occurred	Time occurred

Location (address/block number)	Date reported	Time reported

Loss   ☐ currency, notes   ☐ clothing, furs   ☐ jewelry, precious metals   ☐ firearms   ☐ office equip.   ☐ misc.
☐ TVs, radios, stereos   ☐ household goods   ☐ consumable goods   ☐ livestock   ☐ motor vehs.   ☐ none

WEAPON USED: ☐ Firearm   ☐ Cutting/Stabbing instrument   ☐ Other   ☐ Hands, fist, feet   ☐ Foreign object

☐ Assault: complete weapon line   Assault with intent to commit: ☐ rape   ☐ mayhem
☐ Homicide: complete weapon line   ☐ lewd act   ☐ oral copulation

☐ Robbery: type of location   ☐ street   ☐ gas station   ☐ convenience store   ☐ other
☐ bank   ☐ residence   ☐ other commercial

Complete loss and weapon line   ☐ auto   ☐ commercial   Method of entry: ☐ forcible
☐ Burglary: complete loss line   ☐ residential   ☐ other   ☐ unlawful entry, no force   ☐ att. forcible

☐ Theft: complete loss line   ☐ pickpocket   ☐ purse snatch   ☐ auto access   ☐ auto clout
☐ shoplift   ☐ bicycle   ☐ coin-op device   ☐ other

SUSPECT 1: in custody for offense: ☐ Y   ☐ N   Arrest/Citation #:   ☐ Additional suspects listed on pg. _____

Last name	First	Middle initial	Sex	Race	DOB	Hgt.	Wgt.	Hair	Eyes

Address/School	City, State	Zip	Home phone	Work phone

Other description (clothes, complexion, identifying characteristics, words used):

VEHICLE: ☐ Complainant's   ☐ Suspect's

License number	State	Year	Make	Model	Body type	Color	Hold placed ☐ Y ☐ N

Other identifying information:	Towed to:

Officer	Serial number	Watch	District	Supervisor	Serial number

ADDITIONAL INFORMATION REPORT
ANYWHERE, CA, POLICE DEPARTMENT

Page _____ *of* _____ *Pages* | Beat | Incident number | No. of persons arrested | Case number

PERSON 1: ☐ Complainant ☐ Business

Last name | First | Middle initial | Sex | Race | DOB

Home address | City, State | Zip | Home phone | Work phone

☐ Continuation of: _____ ☐ Offense ☐ Supplemental ☐ Arrest

☐ Supplemental report

CRIME: Common name | Section | Code | Date of original report | Date of this report

Location | Suspect's name | Sex | Race | DOB

Vehicle: License # | State | Year | Make | Model | Color | Operator's license # | State

NARRATIVE:
1. List additional persons, charges, suspects, vehicles.
2. Itemize loss: Give item values and total loss value.

3. Evidence: Itemize, where found, by whom found, disposition
4. Summarize details of incident in logical order.

LOSS:

SUMMARY:

MISSING PERSON REPORTING FORM

1. Check one: ☐ ADULT ☐ JUVENILE

2. Reporting Agency _____

3. Case # _____

5. Department of Justice # _____ 6. NCIC # _____

7. Category: ☐ At Risk ☐ Prior Missing ☐ Sexual Exploitation Expected

8. Name _____ Date/Time Missing _____

9. Alias 1 _____ Alias 2 _____

<table>
<tr><th>4. RECORD TYPE</th></tr>
<tr><td>(Check type best describes)</td></tr>
<tr><td>
☐ Runaway juvenile
☐ Voluntary Missing Adult
☐ Parental/Family Abduction
☐ Non-Family Abduction
☐ Stranger Abduction
☐ Dependent Adult
☐ Lost
☐ Catastrophe
☐ Unknown Circumstances
</td></tr>
</table>

10. Gender	11. Race	12. Hgt.	13. Wgt.	14. Eye Color	15. Hair Color/Length	16. DOB
☐ Male	☐ W ☐ J			☐ Blk ☐ Haz	☐ Blk ☐ Red	
	☐ H ☐ F			☐ Blu ☐ Mar	☐ Bln ☐ Sdy	
☐ Female	☐ B ☐ O			☐ Bro ☐ Pnk	☐ Bro ☐ Wht	
	☐ J ☐ X			☐ Gry ☐ Mul	☐ Gry ☐ XXX	
☐ Unknown	☐ C			☐ Grn ☐ XXX	Length _____	

17. Residence Address _____ City, State _____

18. Location Last Seen _____ ProbableDestination _____

19. Known Associates _____

20. Mental Condition _____

21. SS # _____ FBI # _____ DL # _____

22. Photo Available? ☐ yes ☐ no Age in Photo _____

   Photo/X-ray Waiver Release Signed? ☐ yes ☐ no (Attach photo and signed waiver release form)

23. Scars/Marks/Tattoos (Locate/Describe) _____

24. Skeletal X-rays Available? ☐ yes ☐ no Broken Bones/Missing Organs _____

25. Dental X-rays Available? ☐ yes ☐ no (Attach chart and X-rays.)

   Dentures: ☐ Upper ☐ Lower ☐ Full ☐ Partial

26. Visible Dental Work _____

27. Dentist's Name _____ Phone _____

28. Glasses ☐ Contact Lenses ☐ Clothing Description/Size _____

29. Jewelry Description _____

30. If Vehicle Involved: ☐ S ☐ MP Lic # _____ Make _____ Model _____ Yr _____

---

31. If abduction, did abduction involve movement of missing person in the commission of a crime? yes ☐ no ☐

32. Suspect's Name _____ DOB _____

33. Relationship to Victim _____

---

34. Reporting Party _____ Phone _____

35. Relationship to Missing Person _____ Date Reported _____

36. Additional Information _____

37. Reporting Officer/Agency _____ Phone _____

INCIDENT REPORT

1. Complainant's Name _____

2. Address _____

   _____

3. Telephone (H) _____

   (W) _____

4. Incident (#) _____

5. Date/Time Reported _____

6. Nature of Complaint (Describe in Detail)

_____

_____

_____

_____

_____

_____

_____

_____

_____

_____

7. Reporting Officer _____

STATE PRISON USA
CRIME/INCIDENT REPORT
PART A—COVER SHEET

Page _____ *of* _____ *Pages*

Incident Log Number

FORM 840-A

Institution/Facility	Incident Site/Location		Date Occurred	Time Occurred

Specific Crime/Incident	D.A. Referral ☐ Yes ☐ No	Section/Code/Rule number

☐ SERT Activated? Y or N	☐ Negotiation Team Activated? Y or N	☐ Mutual Aid Requested? Y or N	☐ Media Notified? Y or N

Related Information (Check All That Apply)

Deaths

☐ Staff
☐ Visitor
☐ Inmate
☐ N/A

Cause of Death

☐ Homicide
☐ Suicide
☐ Accidental
☐ Natural
☐ N/A

Assault/Battery

☐ On staff
☐ On visitor
☐ On inmate
☐ Other _____

Type of Assault/Battery

☐ Beating
☐ Shooting
☐ Stabbing
☐ Spearing
☐ Poisoning

☐ Strangling
☐ Slashing
☐ Sexual
☐ Other _____

Serious Injury

☐ Staff
☐ Visitor
☐ Inmate
☐ Accidental
☐ Attempted suicide
☐ Other _____

Inmate Weapons

☐ Firearm
☐ Knife
☐ Spear
☐ Explosive
☐ Projectile
☐ Slashing instrument
☐ Commercial

☐ Stabbing instrument
☐ Hands/Feet
☐ Club/Bludgeon
☐ Caustic substance
☐ Other _____
☐ Inmate manufactured
☐ N/A

Shots Fired

☐ Yes ☐ No

Number
Fired _____

Escapes

☐ With Force
☐ Without force
☐ Attempted

Type Weapon (Staff)

☐ 38-Cal.
☐ Mini-14
☐ H&K .094
☐ Shotgun

☐ 37-mm
☐ Taser
☐ PR-24
☐ Other _____

Suspected Controlled Substance

☐ Heroin/Opiates
☐ Cocaine
☐ Marijunana
☐ Amphetamine
☐ Barbiturate
☐ LSD
☐ PCP
☐ Methamphetamine
☐ Other _____
☐ N/A

Lockdowns

☐ Yes ☐ No
If yes, list affected programs below:

Exceptional Activity

☐ Major disturbance
☐ Inmate strike
☐ Public demonstration
☐ Inmate demonstration
☐ Natural disaster
☐ Environmental hazard
☐ "Special interest inmate"
☐ Weather
☐ N/A

☐ Employee job action
☐ Major power outage
☐ Explosion
☐ Fire
☐ Hostage
☐ Gang involved

☐ Other _____

Description of Crime/Incident:

☐ *Check here if description is continued on Part C.*

Name/Title/Signature of Reporting Staff	Badge/I.D. #	Service (Institution Use)	Date

Authorized Signature/Title (Institution Use)	Date

STATE PRISON USA
CRIME/INCIDENT REPORT
PART B—INVOLVED PARTIES

FORM 840-B

Page ___ of ___ Pages

Institution/Facility	Date Occurred	Time Occurred	Incident Log Number

Inmates

Name (Last, First, MI)				Sex	Ethnicity	Class Score

Check one ☐ Victim ☐ Suspect ☐ Witness	Inmate Number	CII #	FBI #	SS #		PV. RTC?
	Date Received by Prison	Date Received by State	Anticipated Release Date	Date of Birth	Housing Assignment	

Commitment Offenses (Optional)	County of Commitment

Description of Injuries	Prison Gang/Disruptive Group (Validated)

Check All That Apply
☐ Hospitalized ☐ Treated and Released ☐ Refused Treatment ☐ Deceased

Location of Hospital/Treatment

Name (Last, First, MI)				Sex	Ethnicity	Class Score

Check One ☐ Victim ☐ Suspect ☐ Witness	Inmate Number	CII #	FBI #	SS #		PV. RTC?
	Date Received by Prison	Date Received by State	Anticipated Release Date	Date of Birth	Housing Assignment	

Commitment Offenses (Optional)	County of Commitment

Description of Injuries	Prison Gang/Disruptive Group (Validated)

Check All That Apply
☐ Hospitalized ☐ Treated and Released ☐ Refused Treatment ☐ Deceased

Location of Hospital/Treatment

Staff, Visitors, Others

Name (Last, First, MI)	Title	Sex	Ethnicity	Regular Days Off

Check One ☐ Victim ☐ Suspect ☐ Witness	Check One ☐ Staff ☐ Visitor ☐ Other ____	Badge/I.D. #	Post Assignment	I.D. #
		Description of Injuries		

Check All That Apply
☐ Hospitalized ☐ Treated and Released ☐ Refused Treatment ☐ Deceased

Location of Hospital/Treatment

Name (Last, First, MI)	Title	Sex	Ethnicity	Regular Days Off

Check One ☐ Victim ☐ Suspect ☐ Witness	Check One ☐ Staff ☐ Visitor ☐ Other ____	Badge/I.D. #	Post Assignment	I.D. #
		Description of Injuries		

Check All That Apply
☐ Hospitalized ☐ Treated and Released ☐ Refused Treatment ☐ Deceased

Location of Hospital/Treatment

Name (Last, First, MI)	Title	Sex	Ethnicity	Regular Days Off

Check One ☐ Victim ☐ Suspect ☐ Witness	Check One ☐ Staff ☐ Visitor ☐ Other ____	Badge/I.D. #	Post Assignment	I.D. #
		Description of Injuries		

Check All That Apply
☐ Hospitalized ☐ Treated and Released ☐ Refused Treatment ☐ Deceased

Location of Hospital/Treatment

STATE PRISON USA
CRIME/INCIDENT REPORT
PART C—SUPPLEMENTAL

Page ___ of ___ Pages

Incident Log Number

FORM 840-C

Institution/Facility	Date Occurred	Time Occurred

Type of Information

☐ Continuing description of incident (Part A)   ☐ Supplemental information   ☐ Closure report

Narrative:

Name/Title/Signature of Reporting Staff	Badge/I.D. #	Service (Institution Use)	Date
		years months	

Authorized Signature/Title(Institution Use)

STATE PRISON USA
SUPPLEMENTAL TO THE CRIME/INCIDENT REPORT (FORM 839)

Page _____ *of* _____ *Pages*

Name (Last, First, MI)	Badge/I.D. #	Date Occurred	Incident Log Number

Length of Service	I.D. #	Post Description	Time Occurred	Report Date

Days Off	Duty Hours	Incident Location

Description of Incident/Crime	Code of Regulations Section/Rule

Your Role	Witnesses (Preface: S-Staff V-Visitor, O-Other)	Inmates Involved (Preface: S-Suspect, V-Victim, W-Witness)
☐ Primary		
☐ Responder		
☐ Witness		
☐ Victim		
☐ Camera		

Force Used by You	Less Lethal Weapons	Lethal Weapons Number of Rounds Fired	Force Observed by You
☐ Lethal	☐ 37mm _____	☐ Mini-14 _____	☐ Lethal
☐ Less lethal	Serial #	☐ Shotgun _____	☐ Less lethal
☐ Physical	☐ Baton	☐ Handgun _____	☐ Physical
☐ None	☐ OC	☐ Other _____	☐ None
	☐ Other		

Evidence Collected	Evidence Description	Disposition	Weapon	Bio Hazard
☐ Yes			☐ Yes	☐ Yes
☐ No			☐ No	☐ No

Reporting Staff Injured	Description of Injury	Location Treated	Bodily Fluid Exposure
☐ Yes			☐ Yes
☐ No			☐ No

Narrative:

Reporting Staff Signature			Date
Reviewer's Signature	☐ Approved	☐ Clarification Needed	Date

STATE PRISON USA
SUPPLEMENT TO THE CRIME/INCIDENT REPORT (FORM 839-A)

Page _____ *of* _____ *Pages*

Name (Last, First, MI)	Badge/I.D #	Date Occurred	Incident Log Number

☐ Continuation of Report   ☐ Additional information   ☐ Clarification request

Narrative:

Reporting Staff Signature			Date
Reviewer's Signature	☐ Approved	☐ Clarification Needed	Date

STATE PRISON USA
MEDICAL REPORT OF INJURY OR UNUSUAL OCCURRENCE

Name of Hospital

Date

This Section for Inmate Only	Number	Name (Last, First, MI)	Old Housing Location		New Housing Location

This Section for Staff/ Visitor Only	Name (Last, First, MI)		Sex	Age	DOB	Occupation
	Home Address City		State		Zip	Home Phone

Time Occurred	Place Occurred	Time Seen	Mode of Arrival

Brief Resume in Patient's Words of the Circumstances of the Injury or Unusual Occurence

Name of Witnesses, Summaries of Their Stories (Insofar as Available)

RN/MTA's History of Injury/Occurrence

Known Allergies	Date of Last Tetanus

Vital Signs T: BP: P: R:	Time Medical Officer Notified:	Time Medical Officer Arrived:

Comments of Medical Officer

Diagnostic Impression

Treatment

Description of Significant Clinical Laboratory and/or Roentgenologic Findings

Disposition

Estimated or Recommended Number of Days in "Disposition" Status

Prognosis

Signature of RN/MTA   Signature of Medical Officer

STATE PRISON USA
RULES VIOLATION REPORT (FORM 118)

SS Number	Inmate's Name	Release/Board Date	Inst.	Housing No.	Incident Log Number
Violated Rule No.(s)	Specific Acts		Location	Date	Time

Circumstances

Reporting Employee	Date	Assignment	RDOs
Reviewing Supervisor's Signature	Date	Inmate Segregated Pending Hearing Date _____ Loc. _____	

Classified ☐ Administrative ☐ Serious	Offense Division Div.:_____	Date	Classified By	Hearing Referred To ☐ HO ☐ SHO ☐ SC ☐ F

Copies Given Inmate Before Hearing

☐ SP 118	By (Staff's Signature)	Date	Time	Title of Supplement			
☐ Incident Report Log Number	By (Staff's Signature)	Date	Time	By (Staff's Signature)	Date	Time	

Hearing

Referred to	☐ Classification	☐ BPT/NAEA			
Action By		Signature		Date	Time
Reviewed By	Date	Chief Disciplinary Officer's Signature		Date	Time
☐ Copy of SP 118 Given Inmate After Hearing		By		Date	Time

STATE PRISON USA
VICTIM'S CHRONO (FORM 119)

On _____, at approximately _____, you were involved in an act

of _____ at _____. You were deemed the

VICTIM. Inmates _____ and _____ were deemed the suspects, and they should be

considered as ENEMIES.

Orig: Central File
 Cc: Housing Unit File
      CC-I
      Inmate

I. M. Incharge
Correctional Sergeant
Facility IV-B/SHU-ADSEG
State Prison #2

Date _____

Index